CliffsNotes™

The Red Badge of Courage

By Patrick Salerno

IN THIS BOOK

- ■ Learn about the Life and Background of the Author
- ■ Preview an Introduction to the Novel
- ■ Explore themes, character development, and recurring images in the Critical Commentaries
- ■ Examine in-depth Character Analyses
- ■ Acquire an understanding of the novel with Critical Essays
- ■ Reinforce what you learn with CliffsNotes Review
- ■ Find additional information to further your study in the CliffsNotes Resource Center and online at www.cliffsnotes.com

D0483437

Hungry Minds™

Best-Selling Books • Digital Downloads • e-Books • Answer Networks • e-Newsletters • Branded Web Sites • e-Learning

New York, NY • Cleveland, OH • Indianapolis, IN

About the Author

Patrick Salerno has worked as a teacher of language, literature, and composition, and as a curriculum developer in the field of English and language arts.

Publisher's Acknowledgments

Editorial

Project Editor: Mary Goodwin

Acquisitions Editor: Greg Tubach

Editorial Assistant: Michelle Hacker

Glossary Editors: The editors staff of Webster's New World Dictionaries

Production

Indexer: York Production Services, Inc.

Proofreader: York Production Services, Inc.

Hungry Minds Indianapolis Production Services

CliffsNotes™ *The Red Badge of Courage*
Hungry Minds, Inc.
909 Third Avenue
New York, NY 10022
www.hungryminds.com
www.cliffsnotes.com (CliffsNotes Web site)

ISBN: 0-7645-8579-7

Printed in the United States of America

10 9 8 7 6 5 4 3

1V/SW/QT/QS/IN

Distributed in the United States by Hungry Minds, Inc.

Library of Congress Cataloging-in-Publication Data
Slerno, Patrick, 1940-
    CliffNotes, The redbadge of courage /
by Patrick Salerno.
        p.   cm.
    Includes index.
    ISBN 0-7645-8573-7 (alk. paper)
    1. Crane, Stephen, 1871-1900 Red Badge of
Courage--Examinations--Study Guides. 2. United
States--History--Civil War, 1861-1865--Literature
and the war. I. Title: Red badge of courage. II. Title.
PS1449.C85.R3975 2000
813'.4--DC21   00-038847
                                                         CIP

Distributed by CDG Books Canada Inc. for Canada; by Transworld Publishers Limited in the United Kingdom; by IDG Norge Books for Norway; by IDG Sweden Books for Sweden; by IDG Books Australia Publishing Corporation Pty. Ltd. for Australia and New Zealand; by TransQuest Publishers Pte Ltd. for Singapore, Malaysia, Thailand, Indonesia, and Hong Kong; by Gotop Information Inc. for Taiwan; by ICG Muse, Inc. for Japan; by Norma Comunicaciones S.A. for Columbia; by Intersoft for South Africa; by Eyrolles for France; by International Thomson Publishing for Germany, Austria and Switzerland; by Distribuidora Cuspide for Argentina; by LR International for Brazil; by Galileo Libros for Chile; by Ediciones ZETA S.C.R. Ltda. for Peru; by WS Computer Publishing Corporation, Inc., for the Philippines; by Contemporanea de Ediciones for Venezuela; by Express Computer Distributors for the Caribbean and West Indies; by Micronesia Media Distributor, Inc. for Micronesia; by Grupo Editorial Norma S.A. for Guatemala; by Chips Computadoras S.A. de C.V. for Mexico; by Editorial Norma de Panama S.A. for Panama; by American Bookshops for Finland. Authorized Sales Agent: Anthony Rudkin Associates for the Middle East and North Africa.

For general information on Hungry Minds' products and services please contact our Customer Care department; within the U.S. at 800-762-2974, outside the U.S. at 317-572-3993 or fax 317-572-4002.

For sales inquiries and resellers information, including discounts, premium and bulk quantity sales and foreign language translations please contact our Customer Care department at 800-434-3422, fax 317-572-4002 or write to Hungry Minds, Inc., Attn: Customer Care department, 10475 Crosspoint Boulevard, Indianapolis, IN 46256.

For information on licensing foreign or domestic rights, please contact our Sub-Rights Customer Care department at 212-884-5000.

For information on using Hungry Minds' products and services in the classroom or for ordering examination copies, please contact our Educational Sales department at 800-434-2086 or fax 317-572-4005.

Please contact our Public Relations department at 212-884-5163 for press review copies or 212-884-5000 for author interviews and other publicity information or fax 212-884-5400.

For authorization to photocopy items for corporate, personal, or educational use, please contact Copyright Clearance Center, 222 Rosewood Drive, Danvers, MA 01923, or fax 978-750-4470.

Hungry Minds™ is a trademark of Hungry Minds, Inc.

Table of Contents

How to Use This Book

CliffsNotes on *The Red Badge of Courage* supplements the original work, giving you background information about the author, an introduction to the novel, a graphical character map, critical commentaries, expanded glossaries, and a comprehensive index. CliffsNotes Review tests your comprehension of the original text and reinforces learning with questions and answers, practice projects, and more. For further information on Crane and *The Red Badge of Courage*, check out the CliffsNotes Resource Center.

CliffsNotes provides the following icons to highlight essential elements of interest:

Reveals the underlying themes in the work.

Helps you to more easily relate to or discover the depth of a character.

Uncovers elements such as setting, atmosphere, mystery, passion, violence, irony, symbolism, tragedy, foreshadowing, and satire.

Enables you to appreciate the nuances of words and phrases.

Don't Miss Our Web Site

Discover classic literature as well as modern-day treasures by visiting the CliffsNotes Web site at www.cliffsnotes.com. You can obtain a quick download of a CliffsNotes title, purchase a title in print form, browse our catalog, or view online samples.

You'll also find interactive tools that are fun and informative, links to interesting Web sites, tips, articles, and additional resources to help you, not only for literature, but for test prep, finance, careers, computers, and Internet, too. See you at www.cliffsnotes.com!

LIFE AND BACKGROUND OF THE AUTHOR

Personal Background

Stephen Crane was born in a red brick house on Mulberry Place in Newark, New Jersey, on November 1, 1871. Stephen's father was the presiding elder of the Methodist Conference, and, because of this job, the family moved from city to city in New Jersey while Stephen was a child and young boy. Because his parents were aging (his mother was forty-five years old when he was born, and he was their youngest child), he was essentially raised by his sister, Agnes, who was fifteen years older than Crane.

After Crane's father died in 1880, the family continued to move to various places in New Jersey. At one point, Stephen contracted scarlet fever, and the family moved to Port Jervis, New York, a place where Stephen had previously recovered from severe colds. Eventually the Cranes moved to Asbury Park, New Jersey, where Stephen grew into his teen-age years.

Education

Stephen's education was the responsibility of his sister Agnes for the first seven years of his life. He spent much time studying science and literature. He didn't attend school until he was eight years old; however, when he did, he did two years' worth of schoolwork in just six weeks.

Stephen's formal education continued at schools in Port Jervis, New York, and in Asbury Park, New Jersey. While attending school in Asbury Park, Stephen developed into a very good baseball player and writer, and he enjoyed making up words and writing essays. When he was sixteen, he wrote articles with the help of his brother, and he collected information for his mother, who wrote journals for the Methodist Church.

At seventeen, Crane's mother sent him to Claverack College, a military school. Stephen enjoyed his time at Claverack, and the military discipline at the college had no effect on him. Crane didn't complete his studies at Claverack; instead he transferred to Lafayette College in Easton, Pennsylvania. However, at Lafayette, he ultimately flunked out. Finally, Crane enrolled at Syracuse University, but there were far too many distractions at school and in town for him to concentrate on his studies, so in 1891, at the age of twenty, he left the university without completing a degree.

Jobs

In the summer of 1891 in Asbury Park, Crane worked as a reporter for his brother's news business. He also wrote sketches and tales in his spare time. After his mother died, Crane worked briefly in a commercial business and did some freelance writing while living in New York. In 1893, Crane spent his inheritance on publishing *Maggie: A Girl of the Streets.*

After *The Red Badge of Courage* was published in 1895, Crane's reputation as a writer was established. Crane, however, was not content to write without a new challenge, so he accepted a position with the Bacheller-Johnson Syndicate working as a war correspondent. Crane was sent to Cuba to cover a developing conflict between Cuba and Spain. The ship, *Commodore,* on which he set out for Cuba, sustained serious structural damage after running aground and sank. Crane's escape from the sinking ship by rowboat took a great physical toll on him. On the positive side, the experience provided him with the basis for the short story, "The Open Boat."

Crane continued to work as a war correspondent, accepting an assignment from the *New York Journal* to cover a conflict developing between Greece and Turkey in 1897. Following his coverage of the Greco–Turkish conflict, Crane went to England, along with Cora Stewart (also known as Cora Taylor), who became his constant companion.

Crane and Cora resided at Ravensbrook in Oxted, Surrey, located near London. At Ravensbrook, Crane and Cora associated with many literary figures of the day, including Joseph Conrad, Henry James, and H.G. Wells; however, Crane ran into financial difficulties while living there, and, as a result, he again became a war correspondent—this time working for *World,* a Pulitzer publication. He was sent to Florida and then to Cuba to cover the Spanish-American War in 1898. Crane also reported on a conflict with Puerto Rico, but during this time, his health declined, and he made little money.

At the same time, Cora was not doing well in England. Ultimately, Crane returned to England, but he could no longer afford to live at Ravensbrook, so Cora and he moved to Brede Place in Sussex, near Hastings. Their household was still far too large, and their financial difficulties continued. While at Brede, Crane wrote in an attempt to get on sound financial ground, but his health deteriorated, and, on June 5, 1900, he died at Badenweiler, Germany.

Literary Writing

Crane produced many novels, short stories, poems, sketches, and letters during his twenty-nine years of life.

Novels

1893. *Maggie: A Girl of the Streets (A Story of New York)* (by Johnston Smith, a pseudonym used by Crane; republished in 1896 under Crane's name) focuses on social problems and environmental factors which ultimately ruin the life of the main character, Maggie Johnson.

1895. *The Red Badge of Courage: An Episode of the American Civil War* deals with the emotional growth of Henry Fleming from youth to soldier.

1896. *George's Mother* concerns the interrelationships of several characters, including George Kelcey, who aligns himself with a group of losers who engage in a series of questionable behaviors.

1897. *The Third Violet* is the story of the romantic relationship between Billie Hawker and Miss Grace Fanhall and the recognition by Hawker that love can develop if it is given time.

1899. *Active Service: A Novel*, written by Crane primarily to make money, outlines the character of Rufus Coleman, a war correspondent, who saves a professor and his family embroiled in a war, falls in love with the daughter of the professor, rejects the advances of another woman, and brings the family home from the war.

1903. *The O'Ruddy: A Romance* (completed by Robert Barr after Crane's death), observes the behaviors of a main character, O'Ruddy, a man who has little respect for the customs of British culture.

Short Stories

1896. "The Little Regiment and Other Episodes of the American Civil War" looks at the apprehensions and other behaviors of characters in war (Colvert 94).

1898. *The Open Boat and Other Tales of Adventure.* "The Open Boat" is a short story that deals with four characters who escape in a lifeboat from their sinking ship. The story addresses the theme of survival and and is based on Crane's real-life experience with the sinking of the ship *Commodore*.

1899. *The Monster and Other Stories.* "The Monster" addresses themes of compassion and fear.

1900. *Whilomville Stories* (published after Crane's death) is a collection of short stories associated with Crane's life while he was living in several New Jersey cities and in Port Jervis, New York.

1900. *Wounds in the Rain: War Stories:* is a collection of short stories that focuses on Crane's Cuban war experiences.

Poetry

1895. *The Black Riders and Other Lines* is a collection of poems that follow a free verse form and address various content issues, including separation and customs.

1899. *War Is Kind* includes poems with a form and content similar to those in *The Black Riders.*

Other Works

1901. *Great Battles of the World,* which was published after Crane's death, focuses on significant worldwide battles.

1902. *Last Words,* also published after Crane's death, looks at some of Crane's earlier writings.

INTRODUCTION TO THE NOVEL

Introduction

Readers of *The Red Badge of Courage* will note that a sense of confusion and cloudiness pervades the novel. Crane creates this impression intentionally to evoke both the political and military haze that characterized the Civil War, the setting for the novel.

Politically, the Civil War was far from a cut-and-dried conflict to determine the issue of slavery. Two larger issues clouded the political atmosphere of the time, contributing to the division of the Union: states' rights (the southern states considered the institution of slavery one of those rights) and economic development in the South.

The South felt that each state was a sovereign entity and had the right to conduct its business (including having the option to hold slaves) without interference from the federal government. The North, of course, did not support this view. The North believed that all states were subject to the laws of the federal government as determined by each states' representatives operating under the guidance of the Constitution.

Economically, the South was operating in an economy that focused on agriculture, specifically on cotton. As long as the cotton markets in England and France, where textiles were produced, held firm, the southern states producing cotton could retain their way of life. The most-recognized institution in this way of life was the plantation, a farming operation, generally focusing on cotton production, requiring large numbers of people to do the work necessary to turn a profit. Even though machinery, including the cotton gin, was available to help with the planting and the harvesting of commodities, the labor provided by slaves was essential for both small farmers and large plantation owners to operate their businesses successfully. Even southerners who opposed slavery on moral grounds recognized that, economically, they could not operate their farms without this help.

Militarily, the war was often literally fought in a haze. The weapons used by troops on both sides produced a discharge of smoke when fired. As a result, the meadows, forests, roads, and fields, which provided the theater for many battles and skirmishes over the course of several days' fighting, were constantly cloaked in smoke. (Crane refers to this hazy smoke often throughout *The Red Badge of Courage*.) In addition, the slow methods of communication available at that time often made it difficult for either side to tell if a battle was being lost or won. This added to the confusion that characterized the Civil War battlefield.

As for the actual fighting of the war, there were few major victories achieved by either army. Battles often simply reduced the number of men available to each side to keep fighting. This was a war of small battles and skirmishes. The strategy of the commanding officers on both sides was to begin with superior numbers of men, to lose men during the engagement, but hopefully to have more men left than their opponent at the end of the day—and, ultimately, at the end of the war.

Because the Union forces of the North had superior numbers and the potential to replace and to resupply their troops much more efficiently than the Confederate forces of the South, it was inevitable that the sheer weight of numbers would eventually lead to the end of the Civil War: Robert E. Lee's surrender at Appomattox Court House, Virginia, on April 9, 1865.

A Brief Synopsis

The Red Badge of Courage is the story of Henry Fleming, a teenager who enlists with the Union Army in the hopes of fulfilling his dreams of glory.

Shortly after enlisting, the reality of his decision sets in. He experiences tedious waiting, not immediate glory. The more he waits for battle, the more doubt and fear creep into his mind. When he finally engages in his first battle, he blindly fires into the battle haze, never seeing his enemy. As the next enemy assault approaches, Henry's fears of death overwhelm him, and he runs from the field.

Henry continues his retreat for some time, even after he overhears that his regiment repelled the enemy. When he finally slows and rests, he hears the sound of a renewed battle and, ironically, he returns to the battle from which he has fled. He comes upon many wounded men returning from the front to get medical assistance. One of these wounded soldiers, identified as "a tattered soldier," befriends Henry and begins a conversation with him; however, when the tattered soldier asks Henry where he is wounded, Henry evades the question by leaving him and drifting into the crowd of soldiers.

As Henry continues walking with the wounded, he sees a veteran soldier of his company, Jim Conklin, who is mortally wounded. Henry follows Jim, and, eventually, the tattered soldier joins them. When Jim suddenly collapses and dies, Henry is devastated. The tattered soldier again asks Henry about his wound. Again, Henry can't explain that he has no wound, so he leaves the disoriented, wounded, tattered soldier stumbling in the field.

Henry anguishes over his lack of courage, but he can't overcome the guilt and self-hatred that stop him from returning to his regiment. He hears the noise of a battle and sees reinforcement troops heading toward the front. As he watches, the battle turns against the Union forces, and many of the men begin to retreat. Henry gets caught up in their retreat. He tries to stop a retreating soldier to find out what is happening; however, the soldier only wants to get away, so he hits Henry over the head with his rifle, leaving Henry with a serious head wound. He is dazed by the blow and wanders back through the woods. Henry is then befriended by a cheery soldier who returns him to his regiment.

Henry fears being ridiculed by his comrades on his return, but when he enters his camp, two soldiers, Wilson and Simpson, see his injury and immediately begin ministering to him. They assume that Henry was hurt in battle; however, Simpson asks Henry about his whereabouts, and Henry can't answer.

As the regiment prepares to move out, Wilson asks Henry to return a packet of letters that he gave Henry before the first battle. (Wilson feared that he was going to die in battle, and he wanted Henry to give the letters to his family.) Henry realizes that Wilson was also afraid of battle, and Henry is overjoyed to think that he now has power, and a weapon, to use to hold over somebody else's head. This knowledge gives Henry courage and restores his confidence.

Henry converts his fear of the enemy into anger and becomes a leader, fighting boldly at the side of his lieutenant. Henry becomes such a confident, assertive, aggressive soldier that, ironically, he becomes a fighting machine himself. Henry resolves his guilt over abandoning the tattered soldier by deciding to use the memory of this selfish, uncaring act to keep himself humble—to control any egotism he feels because of his now strong fighting ability.

When Henry's regiment is chosen to charge the enemy, Henry leads the charge with the lieutenant, and, eventually, he even assumes the role of color bearer for the regiment after the color sergeant is killed.

Henry's transformation from a fearful, lost, doubting youth, to a courageous, confident, duty-bound soldier is the essence of the novel. It is the story of the growth of a young man from innocence to maturity.

List of Characters

Henry Fleming. Henry, the protagonist of the novel, is a young Union soldier enlistee. He enters the army with strong romantic feelings about war. After experiencing the realities of army life, he becomes plagued by doubts and fears. As the novel progresses, Henry overcomes his fears and guilt to become one of the fiercest, most aggressive soldiers in the regiment. Henry conquers doubt and accepts duty by showing the confidence and courage required to be a soldier.

The Loud Soldier (Wilson). Wilson is Henry's friend. He takes care of Henry's head injury. Wilson changes from a very pragmatic, somewhat arrogant, do-your-job soldier, to a compassionate veteran who shows care and concern for his comrades. Wilson gives Henry a packet of his personal letters to be sent home if he should die in battle. Henry considers these letters a sign of weakness, and, ironically, he uses these letters as an aid to restoring his own courage.

The Tall Soldier/The Spectral Soldier (Jim Conklin). Jim is a positive, confident Union soldier who lifts the spirits of the younger soldiers. However, Jim is mortally wounded in the first battle, and Henry watches him die in the field. His death has a profound, depressing effect on Henry.

The Lieutenant (Lt. Hasbrouck). The lieutenant leads Henry's company with courage and conviction. He represents the confident Union officers who are always shown as strong leaders. The lieutenant is so pleased with Henry's fighting ability that he calls him a "wild cat," a term which brings great pride to Henry.

The Tattered Soldier. The tattered, wounded soldier twice asks Henry about how he was wounded. This questioning angers Henry, and he leaves the tattered soldier wandering in the same field where Jim dies. Henry uses the episode with the tattered soldier to remind him that he must always be humble.

Henry's Mother. After Henry enlists against her wishes, Henry's mother doesn't mention anything about glorious battles and heroic actions (to Henry's disappointment). Instead, she advises him to do the right thing and not to be a shirking child.

The Corporal (Simpson). When Henry returns to the regiment, Simpson, a corporal in the regiment, asks Henry the question, "Where were yeh?" Simpson's question angers Henry because he can't answer the question honestly.

The Cheery Soldier. The cheery soldier befriends Henry after he is struck on the head by a retreating soldier. The cheery soldier also returns Henry to his regiment.

The Colonel (Colonel MacChesnay). The colonel is the commander of Henry's regiment. When a general criticizes the regiment's efforts after an offensive, the colonel doesn't defend the troops' actions; instead, he says, "Oh, well, general, we went as far as we could."

The General (the Officer in Charge of Henry's Brigade). This officer selects Henry's regiment to take the offensive in support of Whiterside and his troops. After the regiment returns, unsuccessfully, from the offensive, he criticizes the regiment. He calls Henry's regiment "a lot of mud diggers." This comment motivates Henry to prove that the general is wrong.

The Red-Bearded Officer. He motivates the troops to charge the enemy's position in support of Whiterside, but he shows disappointment and anger when the charge stalls. However, he also shows disdain for another regiment's soldiers who criticize Henry's regiment for not achieving their objective in the charge.

Whiterside (a Union Officer). Whiterside's need for additional battlefield support prompts the general to select Henry's regiment to launch a charge against the enemy.

The Captain. He is a dedicated officer in Henry's regiment who is killed in the first battle.

Character Map

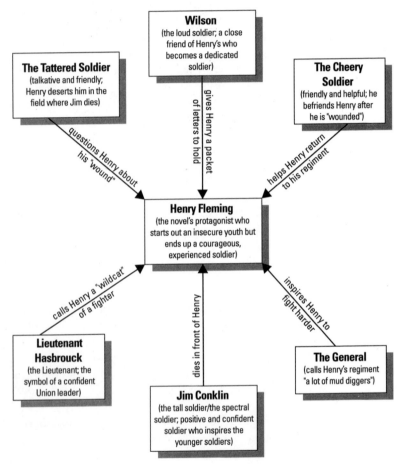

Wilson
(the loud soldier; a close friend of Henry's who becomes a dedicated soldier)

The Tattered Soldier
(talkative and friendly; Henry deserts him in the field where Jim dies)

The Cheery Soldier
(friendly and helpful; he befriends Henry after he is "wounded")

questions Henry about his "wound"

gives Henry a packet of letters to hold

helps Henry return to his regiment

Henry Fleming
(the novel's protagonist who starts out an insecure youth but ends up a courageous, experienced soldier)

calls Henry a "wildcat" of a fighter

dies in front of Henry

inspires Henry to fight harder

Lieutenant Hasbrouck
(the Lieutenant; the symbol of a confident Union leader)

Jim Conklin
(the tall soldier/the spectral soldier; positive and confident soldier who inspires the younger soldiers)

The General
(calls Henry's regiment "a lot of mud diggers")

CRITICAL COMMENTARIES

Chapter 1

Summary

As the novel opens, the soldiers of a regiment are waiting for battle. After one of the men, a tall soldier, suggests that a battle is imminent, other soldiers argue against the notion. One of the young soldiers, Henry, a private, returns to the hut where the regiment is camped and thinks about war. He recalls his desire to enlist in the army, his mother's refusal to support the idea, and his eventual decision to enlist over her objections. He remembers the reactions of his schoolmates to his enlistment, his mother's advice to him when he leaves for the army, the reception given to his regiment as it moved toward Washington, the tedious waiting, and the frightening tales of war told by various veterans in the regiment. His mind struggles with the question of what he will do when—and if—an actual battle takes place.

As he contemplates the prospects of battle, "a little panic-fear" grows in his mind, and, suddenly, he jumps from his bunk and begins to pace the floor. Other soldiers enter the hut, and the discussion about the prospect of an impending battle continues. The tall soldier, Jim Conklin, who brings the news that a battle is certain, comments on how he expects the new soldiers to react and on how he himself will react under fire.

Commentary

The overriding impression of this first chapter is one of conflict. The Union soldiers await a physical battle with the Confederate troops in the area. The imminent external conflict is paralleled by the fight raging in Henry's mind. As the book opens, the reader sees the main character, a soldier waiting for his first battle, ironically engaged in an internal conflict with his own thoughts.

Theme

The theme of the struggle between confidence and fear and doubt is a major portion of Chapter 1. Henry is so sure about the glory awaiting him in war that he enlists despite his mother's wishes. His romantic vision of war convinces him that he must enlist in the army. However, this confidence quickly fades, and even in this first chapter, Henry struggles between his romanticized assurance and his lack of confidence about his untested performance.

Henry is almost entirely introspective in this first chapter, which sets the stage for following Henry's thoughts and emotions throughout the novel. The reader can anticipate seeing Henry, a young man who initially turns inward when confronted by grave issues, develop the confidence necessary to be a frontline soldier. For Henry, initially, this introspective behavior overrides his reasoning ability, and only time and experience will help him face the realities of war. A part of this maturing process involves Henry's moving away from the questioning of his behavior and motivations, of his comrades' behavior and motivations, and of the officers' decisions and plans for battle.

Theme

In addition, the themes of duty and honor surface in Chapter 1. Henry recalls the wonderful sensation of honor and pride that he feels as his regiment is showered with attention on their way to Washington. Clearly, Henry prizes valor and feels a sense of honor and commitment toward his regiment; however, these valiant feelings are almost completely overshadowed by fear and lack of confidence. Again, the reader sees Henry as a youth with many opposing feelings and thoughts. This issue of honor, especially as it relates to being courageous under fire, or running from a fight, is a major plot motivator throughout the book.

Other characters presented in Chapter 1 reflect the conflict between youth and experience. The experienced soldiers may be skeptical of the skills and commitment of the untested, new recruits. The new enlistees may doubt the veracity of the tales told by the veterans. Both groups know that, at some point, the reality of a battle will resolve this issue.

Style & Language

The use of dialect is established in Chapter 1, and it continues throughout the book. The soldiers' conversations reflect the dialect of the speakers. This use of dialogue allows the reader to identify characters through their language, as well as their other behaviors, and allows Crane to contrast the colloquialisms and regionalisms stated with the more philosophical ideas presented through the thoughts of the characters. For example, when Henry contemplates on how he will react in battle, Crane states that "He [Henry] lay in his bunk pondering on it. He tried to mathematically prove to himself that he would not run from a battle." When the topic of battle comes up in conversation in the bunkhouse (the hut), the tall soldier (Jim) responds to Henry's question of whether there will be a battle by saying in very colloquial speech, "Of course there is. You jest wait 'til tomorrow, and you'll see one of the biggest battles ever was. You jest wait."

Thinking about war in philosophical terms while lying in one's bunk does not require one to face war realistically. Crane gets to the reality of war through the use of dialect and colloquialisms of the soldiers, those men who must fight and face death. For them, war is not a philosophical discussion; it is a battle for survival, and the language which they use reflects that understanding. Crane's use of dialect allows the reader to separate the philosophy of war from the reality which the men will face in battle.

Literary Device

Stylistically, Crane develops images through the use of figurative language, particularly personification (a type of metaphor which gives an inanimate object, a thing, or an idea the characteristics or qualities of a person), in this chapter and throughout the novel. For example, in the passage, "The cold passed reluctantly from the earth, and the retiring fogs revealed an army stretched out on the hills, resting," the cold, the fog, and the army are described as persons with specific behaviors, feelings, and needs. The use of personification and other forms of figurative language brings Crane's images of war to life.

Crane's use of both figurative language and rhetorical devices is constant throughout the text, primarily because he wants the reader to see that the beauty of nature will prevail, no matter what types of negative behaviors humanity introduces into the environment (in this case, waging war). Nature's beauty provides a contrast of beauty to the drabness, darkness, and destruction which humanity introduces into the environment.

Glossary

Here, and in the following sections, difficult words and phrases are explained.

private an enlisted man of the two lowest ranks in the U.S. Army.

corporal the lowest-ranking noncommissioned officer, just below a sergeant.

omen a thing or happening supposed to foretell a future event, either good or evil; augury.

returning with his shield or on it a reference to the ancient Greek idea that the only honorable way to return from battle is to be holding your shield or to be carried back on it.

a shirking child a child who neglects an obligation.

pickets soldiers stationed at an outpost to guard the troops from surprise attack.

Yank a Yankee, a Union soldier.

Huns a warlike Asiatic people who, led by Attila and others, invaded eastern and central Europe in the fourth and fifth century A.D.; here, a reference to the rebel forces made by veteran Union soldiers to frighten the new recruits.

haversack a canvas bag for carrying rations, generally worn over one shoulder.

Richmond the capital of Virginia and of the Confederacy.

Johnnies Confederate soldiers.

fresh fish a derogatory term for new soldiers.

regiment a military unit consisting of two or more battalions and forming a basic element of a division. (*U.S. Army* A battalion is a tactical unit made up of three or more companies, batteries, or analogous units: it is normally commanded by a lieutenant colonel and is the basic building unit of a division. *Mil.* A division is an army unit larger than a regiment and smaller than a corps, to which various numbers and types of battalions can be attached as required.)

Chapter 2

Summary

The regiment continues to rest, and Henry remains deep in his own thoughts, contemplating the possibility of battle and questioning his ability to cope with battle when it comes. The other soldiers, in Henry's view, don't seem to share his worries. Indeed, some are jovial and appear to be excited about the prospect of engaging in combat. Henry concludes that his comrades are all heroes without fear, but on further reflection, he feels that, perhaps, they are all as fearful as he, yet they suppress that fear.

Early one morning several days later, the regiment stands ready to move out. As the regiment waits in the predawn, a horseman brings the news to move the regiment to a new position. As the night turns to morning, the regiment crosses the hills. At the end of the day's march, the regiment camps in a field. Henry rests, and as he rests, he thinks of his life on the farm and wishes he were there. His thoughts are interrupted when one of the loud, boisterous soldiers, Wilson, walks by, and Henry begins a conversation with him.

Wilson speaks confidently of the upcoming battle. When Henry asks him if he might run when the fighting begins, he laughs the comment off. However, when Henry presses him on the issue, Wilson angrily challenges Henry's authority to question his bravery. That night, Henry falls into a sleep disturbed by doubts and fears.

Commentary

Character Insight

Chapter 2 continues to focus on Henry's internal conflict about his bravery, or lack thereof. Henry is fixated on proving his courage, and his obsession with the issue causes him to become distant and removed from the other members of the regiment. He feels like an outcast, as if he is strangely not like the other soldiers. Henry's feelings of isolation foreshadow his physical separation and retreat from the regiment later in the novel.

Style & Language

A mainstay of Crane's stylistic techniques is his use of imagery to develop the mood of foreboding which permeates the novel. Chapter 2 contains several good examples of this imagery. Selected vocabulary words, similes (the comparing of one entity to another dissimilar entity, usually using the words, "like" or "as"), metaphors (the comparing of one entity to another, dissimilar entity by suggesting that the first entity is the other entity), and other figures of speech develop this somber, dark mood. For example, Henry lives in a "mystic gloom," a phrase which exemplifies Crane's talent in selecting the perfect words to express a mood. An excellent example of Crane's use of simile occurs in his description of the regiments: they "were like two serpents crawling from the cavern of the night."

Imagery for the impending battle is also developed using similar techniques. Fire and monster imagery combines with dark and gloom imagery. The battle is "the blaze" and "a monster"; the combatants are "serpents crawling from hill to hill"; Henry's regiment is a "blasting host" (a killing machine); "red eyes" (enemy campfires) watch across rivers. All these images, which are metaphors, create an oppressive mood of foreboding.

Literary Device

Another dimension of Crane's writing that becomes obvious in Chapter 2 is the use of the third person terms for major characters. The tall soldier (Jim), the loud soldier (Wilson), and the youth (Henry) are identified in this manner to allow Crane greater latitude in making objective comments about the characters' behaviors. Only through conversations between and among characters are characters' real names revealed. Not identifying characters by name engages the reader's imagination to draw pictures and conclusions about these characters. By appealing to the imagination in this way, the reader is drawn closer to the characters.

In Chapters 1 and 2, Crane uses various characters to show the reader different responses to the central issue of the novel—bravery under fire. The practical confidence of Wilson contrasts with the all-encompassing doubt that Henry experiences. At the same time, the reader recalls the somewhat humorous, carefree, easy-come-easy-go attitude of Jim Conklin's reply to Henry at the close of Chapter 1 after Henry asks him if he might run when the battle starts. These responses represent the spectrum of feelings which combatants in war may feel. That Crane chooses to focus on Henry's response to war, that of fear and doubt, implies that this is a response that all soldiers have to war at one time in their careers.

Glossary

a blue demonstration the perception that, at this point, the regiment is preparing for a protest rather than for a battle.

gods of traditions behaviors that are expected with certain activities.

colonel a high-ranking military officer ranking below a brigadier general.

company wags humorous soldiers; jokesters.

brigade a unit of the U.S. Army comprising two or more regiments.

dregs bitter-tasting particles of solid matter that settle to the bottom of a bottle of wine.

Napoleon Bonaparte 1769-1821; French military leader and emperor of France (1804-1815); here, Wilson's sarcastic response to Henry for questioning his courage.

the red eyes (also described as red blossoms) the camp fires of the enemy as seen across the river.

Chapter 3

Summary

The regiment rests during the second day of their march, and that night, they cross a bridge and sleep again. On the morning of the third day, they again move out and march to a forest. They remain there for several days.

On "one gray dawn" the whole regiment begins to run as if running toward a battle, but there is no battle. The regiment walks and then halts, and the soldiers continue to move from place to place. There is much grumbling among the men because of the constant walking and stopping. On occasion, the regiment sees skirmishers in the distance and hears the sounds of battle. The regiment comes upon a dead soldier, and Henry tries "to read in dead eyes the answer to the Question." Henry continues to challenge, internally, the intelligence of the generals who are directing the troop movements, and he feels hatred toward the lieutenant who enforces troop discipline by keeping him marching in rank.

Henry considers that if he were to die quickly, he could end his anguish. The regiment comes upon a battle in the distance, and the men begin to prepare for battle. As the chapter ends, the loud soldier (Wilson) tells Henry that he expects to die in battle, and he hands Henry a packet which he asks Henry to take to his family.

Commentary

Throughout most of Chapter 3, the major characters behave just as they have in Chapters 1 and 2.

Jim continues to accept everything that happens as part of a grand plan. He shows no worry. In Crane's words, "The philosophical, tall soldier measured a sandwich of cracker and pork and swallowed it in a nonchalant manner." And later in the chapter Crane writes, "He [Jim] accepted new environments and circumstances with great coolness, eating from his haversack at every opportunity."

Character
Insight

Henry's characterization is also consistent. His fears persist, and his self-doubt hasn't changed. His reactions to his environment—both to the countryside and the Confederate soldiers—become predictable. For example, when the regiment covered the same ground in both the morning and afternoon, Henry was comfortable the second time around because he had been there before. He knew the land. As Crane says of Henry, "The landscape then ceased to threaten the youth. He had been close to it and become familiar with it." However, as the troops entered fresh fields, Crane says, ". . . his [Henry's] fears of stupidity and incompetence reassailed him." At one point his fears become so great that he wants to die so that he can silence his doubts. Henry's thoughts in this chapter continue to develop the themes of fear, doubt, duty, confidence, and glory, themes which have been apparent from the opening chapter.

Henry's reaction to entering new territory is predictable, especially considering that, for any soldier, entering new ground may bring combat. The troop movement described in this chapter is especially trying for Henry because entering of new ground could bring with it his first taste of combat. It is only natural, therefore, that a new recruit would be very fearful of new territory and very comfortable covering old ground. The issue here is fear of the unknown, a fear common to all people, and soldiers face a higher price for venturing into the unknown than do regular citizens. As a soldier gains experience in covering new territory, he gains control of his fear. This pattern of reducing fear through gaining experience characterizes Henry's transition throughout the novel.

Henry's youthful confidence reasserts itself in a strange way in Chapter 3. At one point, Henry fears even the shadows in the woods, and he concludes that he and his comrades are trapped. He blames the generals for allowing this to happen. Henry thinks, "The generals were idiots to send them marching into a regular pen." He feels that "There was but one pair of eyes in the corps" (his). This implies, of course, that Henry thinks that he knows more about waging war than the officers do. This observation comes from a soldier who has never been in a battle. Even so, this reaction is probably not unusual for a very nervous, worried young man who continues to anticipate an impending battle and all the dangers associated with it.

Jim and Henry's behaviors in this chapter simply continue what has been established about them in previous chapters. However, at the end of the chapter, Wilson does something that shows the reader a different side of his character. Hearing the sounds of battle, Wilson speaks openly about his fears of death. This is the first time in the book that a character other than Henry expresses fear about the impending battle, and the reader sees that Henry is not truly alone in his thoughts.

Wilson's comments represent the comments of all men in battle. If Wilson the pragmatic, somewhat boastful soldier fears death, then it follows that this fear probably resides in all soldiers facing battle. If this is the case, then this fear is not a sign of weakness; on the contrary, it is probably a sign of normalcy. This revelation is important for soldiers who equate fear with weakness and, as a result, begin to develop self-doubts. At this point, Henry is such a person, and Wilson's comments provide some solace for Henry.

Stylistically, Crane again uses metaphor and other kinds of figurative language to develop the images which grasp the reader's mind. The regiment is sometimes a person, sometimes a monster, sometimes a reptile. The reader loses sight of the fact that the regiment is a unit of individual men. This continued use of personification creates the feeling that a battle is a battle between regimental monsters. For example, Crane describes the regiment's crossing of a river in animal terms when he writes, "The regiment slid down a bank and wallowed across a little stream." These references and images symbolize the monsters within Henry—monsters of fear, doubt, and loneliness, which he continues to try to suppress, but which don't retreat. Wilson's death revelation provides additional fuel for the growth of these monsters.

Crane uses animal imagery to describe the elements of war, including armies and weapons. The use of animal imagery allows Crane to separate the inhumanity of the war animal from the humanity of the individual soldier. Indeed, an army (the animal) has appendages, including divisions, regiments, and companies. These appendages work together to provide a system for this animal, this monster, to do battle with an enemy animal. Crane uses this animal imagery to contrast the army with the individual soldier. The animal seems to have no concerns for anything; individual soldiers show all emotions. The soldier must cast aside his individuality to become a part of the animal needed to do battle.

Glossary

skirmish/skirmishers a brief fight or encounter between small groups of troops/the troops who take part in a skirmish.

perambulating veterans strolling troops.

the colors the flag.

the Question the question which all soldiers face: What will death be like?

the generals the highest-ranking officers, above the colonels.

the lieutenant an officer ranking above a second lieutenant and below a captain; here, a first lieutenant.

battery a set of heavy guns; cannons.

Chapter 4

Summary

The entire brigade finally stops near a grove of trees, and the soldiers watch other regiments of other brigades do battle ahead of them. As they watch and wait, they share rumors regarding how other companies, regiments, battalions, individual soldiers, and officers have been doing in battles. There is disagreement as to how effective some have been and how strong the enemy is.

The lieutenant of Henry's company is wounded while waiting and is treated by the company's captain; at the same time, the front line troops seem to be in disarray. Officers of that brigade are both cursing and cajoling their men to keep fighting, but there are many in retreat. The troops in the reserve brigade, including those in Henry's regiment, watch the action with both awe and fear. As yet, however, the enemy causing all this chaos hasn't been seen.

Commentary

Theme

Crane continues to develop the theme of fear by allowing the soldiers to comment on rumors. For example, one soldier says, "They say Perry has been driven in with big loss" and "Hannises' battery is took." The reader also sees the battle through the eyes of a novice and shares the fears of the youth. The reader shares Henry's curiosity as he watches the frontline troops do battle.

Crane's technique of allowing the reader to watch the battle through the eyes of another in some ways limits the reader's perspective, but, in other ways, it increases the concern for personal safety. The theme of fear, in this case fear of the unknown, grows because the soldiers don't see, and have not, as yet, seen the enemy—the force, the monster, causing all this chaos, and the reader, as a result, hasn't yet seen the monster, either. Indeed, the fear of the unknown is greater than the fear of facing the enemy directly. This fear of the unknown is a normal human behavior, one with which all people can identify, and, as a result, the reader empathizes with Henry.

Glossary

a company a body of troops, specifically, the lowest administrative unit, as of infantry, normally composed of two or more platoons and a headquarters.

rebel army the Confederate Army.

bushwhacker a name given to Confederate soldiers by Union soldiers.

a storm banshee in folklore, a banshee is a female spirit believed to wail outside a house as a warning that a death will occur soon in the family; here, it refers to the shrieking sound of the artillery shells coming in over the heads of the troops.

captain an officer ranking above a first lieutenant and below a major.

color sergeant the sergeant in charge of carrying the flag for a unit.

the composite monster the enemy army.

Chapter 5

Summary

As Henry waits for his regiment to enter the battle, he thinks about earlier days and people he has known. His thoughts are interrupted by the words, "Here they come!" The enemy initiates its charge, and the battle rages as Henry's regiment tries to repel the enemy forces. Henry becomes a member of a fighting team, and he shows great strength and resolve as he loads, fires, and reloads his rifle—even while others are being wounded and killed around him. The officers encourage all the troops to keep firing, and they reprimand those whose fear overcomes them. Henry doesn't apparently suffer from these fears. He continues to fire and reload, to fire and reload—even wishing that he could do so faster. Then the fighting stops, and the enemy retreats. The regiment holds its ground, and the soldiers are jubilant. Henry suddenly feels suffocated by the smoke, by the event. He takes a drink from his canteen to clear his head.

As Henry surveys the field, he realizes that other battles are continuing even as he rests. He recognizes that his regiment's "battle" was but one small skirmish in a whole series of conflicts. He is encouraged by the beauty of the flags blowing in the wind, and he marvels at the brightness of the sky and land even in the midst of the smoke and chaos.

Commentary

Once Henry hears the words, "Here they come!" he is a changed soldier. Henry seems to totally forget the fears that have almost overwhelmed him up to this point in the novel.

Character
Insight

Henry transforms from a fearful, doubtful, questioning recruit to a confident, aggressive, regimental soldier in only one battle. Henry stands side by side with other recruits and with experienced veterans—all working together for a single cause—to hold the line. As Crane tells the reader, "He [Henry] became not a man but a member. He felt that something of which he was a part—a regiment, an army, a cause, a country—was in a crisis. He was welded into a common personality which was dominated by a single desire." This is a phenomenon common to all human beings. In times of trouble, people find strength in numbers. Henry is no exception. He stands up in battle, fights, and helps the regiment repel the enemy.

Henry' reaction is the reaction of any soldier. If he is to fight, he must be energized and focused. This attack by the enemy has angered and exasperated him, and, as a result, he wants to remove this source of irritation, in this case the enemy. His fears are surpassed by his anger and frustration, and he fires his rifle repeatedly as a result. It is not until the enemy retreats that he realizes what he and his comrades have accomplished.

Character Insight

Henry's ability to recognize that the battle just completed is but one part of a larger war is significant because it shows Henry getting outside himself and looking at the bigger picture. To this point, Henry has been very focused on himself. This ability to get beyond himself and to see the larger issues shows a developing maturity on the part of Henry—something not seen before in him.

Theme

After the skirmish, as he rests, Henry drinks, and he observes the beauty and brightness of the sun and sky. He recognizes nature's beauty even in this chaos. He marvels at nature's patience with man. Through these insights, Crane creates the impression that nature is in control of man. Henry's behavior from the beginning of the book is natural behavior: his fears, his doubts, his anger, his longing. Then, when he engages in battle, he comes to realize that he is a member of a group, and that there is strength in group membership. This behavior is part of the natural order of human life, and Crane points out that nature plays a prominent role in the lives of people and in this work.

Literary Device

Crane also continues to use figurative language to create powerful images in the mind of the reader. This chapter includes several similes which describe the battle vividly, including, "his eyeballs were about to crack like hot stones"; "The man at the youth's elbow was babbling something soft and tender like the monologue of a babe"; and "The guns squatted in a row like savage chiefs."

Also, Crane uses symbolism as the reader sees the flag representing inspiration, hope, and beauty—almost equally with nature—in this chapter. Crane tells the reader that "The youth felt the old thrill at the sight of the emblem. They [the flags] were like beautiful birds strangely undaunted in a storm." The flag takes on added importance for Henry because in Chapter 19, the color sergeant, the flag bearer, is killed in battle, and, in Chapter 20, Henry, after scuffling with Wilson to win the right to hold the flag, assumes the responsibilities of flag bearer, exhibiting great enthusiasm and courage in that role.

Glossary

red rage great anger.

so much devilment the chaos of war.

Chapter 6

Summary

Henry and the other soldiers are exultant about their first triumph in battle. Indeed, Henry is in "an ecstasy of self-satisfaction." He is proud of his efforts and of his comrades' efforts. But, suddenly, a shout is heard, "Here they come again!" The regiment is surprised, and Henry's previous fears return to plague him. He imagines that this enemy isn't an enemy of men but of machines. As he begins to reload his rifle for the inevitable battle, he no longer sees an enemy of men, but a group of monsters consumed with the goal of devouring him. As his imagination continues to run wild, he notes that one or two of his comrades have dropped their guns and fled.

As the "red and green monster" comes closer, Henry throws down his gun and runs "like a rabbit." As he flees from the front line, he notes that the batteries continue to fire. He overhears the conversation of a general and his initial irritation with the deployment of his troops, which is followed by a show of exuberance as he hears that the line has held. The general eagerly exhorts his commanders to go after the enemy "to go in—everlastingly—like blazes—anything." As the chapter ends, the general is so happy that he does "a little carnival of joy on horseback."

Commentary

In this chapter, Crane shows Henry's instability as he goes from a state of euphoria after repelling the enemy's charge in the first battle to a state of total panic at the beginning of a second battle.

Henry can't understand how the enemy can possibly regroup to do battle again so quickly. Crane reveals Henry's confusion in these words, "He [Henry] waited, as if he expected the enemy to suddenly stop, apologize, and retire bowing. It was all a mistake." He can't imagine that his regiment could, or would, do such a thing, and he speculates that the enemy can't really be a group of individual men similar to the men in his regiment. His thoughts show his increasing fear of the enemy as

Crane tells the reader that "He began to exaggerate the endurance, the skill, and the valor of those who were coming. Himself reeling from exhaustion, he was astonished beyond measure at such persistency. They must be machines of steel."

Literary
Device

Henry's deteriorating physical condition—"His neck was quivering with nervous weakness and the muscles of his arms felt numb and bloodless"—foreshadows his mental collapse. When the soldier next to him drops his rifle and runs, Henry's imagination takes total control over his reasoning ability, and he runs.

It is also interesting to note that Crane's characterizations of the Union officers are consistent and believable. The officers of all ranks don't panic; they are in control; they lead their troops and exhort their units to fight aggressively. For example, when the enemy begins its second offensive, the reader sees that "The lieutenant sprang forward bawling" (hollering at his troops to continue fighting). Henry is surprised at this officer's singular focus and courage.

As Henry runs away from the front, he comes upon a meeting of officers, and he overhears the general discussing strategy with the other officers. There is no panic in the general's voice when he says, "Tompkins go over and see Taylor and tell him to halt his brigade in the edge of th' woods." And later, when the officers hear that the regiment has repelled the enemy's offensive, the general says, "Yes, by heavens, they've held 'im! . . . We'll wallop 'im now. We've got 'em sure." These comments show clearly the confidence and courage of the officers. Indeed, it is only when Henry overhears the rational observations of the general that he is able to suppress his panic and gain some level of stability.

Style &
Language

Crane's images, as seen through Henry's thoughts, make it clear that Henry has lost all his rational powers, and he is in a total state of panic. Crane uses figurative language, including metaphor, personification, and simile, to create powerful mental images. The enemy soldiers are metaphorically "machines of steel," "redoubtable dragons," and "a red and green monster"; the men who were nearest the battle would make the "initial morsels for the dragons"; "the shells flying past him have rows of cruel teeth that grinned at him." These images show that Henry's perception of the enemy has gone wild.

Crane again uses figurative language in this chapter to develop nature images related to war and to the beauty of nature for nature's sake. The reader should note the use of metaphor in the image, "the shells looked to be strange war flowers bursting into fierce bloom," and the use of personification in the line, "The sore joints of the regiment creaked as it painfully floundered into position." The reader can observe Crane's continued use of similes to make comparisons in these examples: the rebel forces were "running like pursued imps" and Henry, at first, "ran like a rabbit" and, later, "like a blind man."

Also the reader sees the continuing use of images of nature, particularly color images, to make the setting more vivid. Examples include "The clouds were tinged an earthlike yellow in the sunrays and in the shadow were a sorry blue" and the flag was "sun-touched." Sun and clouds—images of nature—play a role in setting a tone of contrasts. The natural, innocent, colorful beauty of the sun and clouds provides a backdrop for the unnatural actions of men in war.

Glossary

to chant a paean   to sing a hymn of thanksgiving and praise.

Chapter 7

Summary

Henry continues his flight from the front line even after he learns that his comrades have repelled the charge of the enemy. As he continues to retreat, he rationalizes his flight by first suggesting that his comrades were fools to stay and fight. Indeed, if they weren't wise enough to see that their position was going to be overrun, wasn't he just being wiser to run? According to his reasoning, his flight was the wise thing to do. As his retreat continues, he becomes angrier with his regiment, and he reinforces his anger by mentally criticizing his comrades for their willingness to stay.

He further rationalizes his retreat when he sees a squirrel scamper away from him as he moves through the forest. He thinks that all creatures in nature move to safety when their existence is threatened. As a result, he rationalizes that he was only doing the natural thing when he fled because he feared that his existence was in question.

As he moves further away from the front, he sees a thicket which might offer him some protection. He squeezes through the branches, and he comes face to face with a dead soldier. Henry immediately backs out of the thicket and continues his retreat.

Commentary

Character
Insight

In this chapter, Crane develops Henry's character by allowing him to rationalize his behavior. After he retreats from the battle and the wild fear that caused him to run, he returns to a state of reason and relative stability. Henry dismisses any notion that his running was not the right thing to do by rationalizing that his comrades were fools to stay and die. Henry is angry with his comrades when he learns that they were not annihilated, but, rather, were victorious in battle. Henry assumes that they are fools to continue to press their luck.

Henry rationalizes his behavior by thinking that his decision to run in the face of an overwhelming enemy force (at least in his mind) was the only rational decision he could make because, by taking this action, he would be available to fight and continue his duty another day while his comrades would be dead. The fact that this annihilation did not happen can be attributed only to luck, according to Henry's reasoning.

In his isolation, Henry attempts to find justification for his actions in nature. Henry contemplates that even the smallest of nature's creatures (in this chapter, a squirrel) knows when to run for safety. Shouldn't the most intelligent of nature's creatures, a human being, do the same? The reader should note Henry's decision to rationalize his behavior when the behavior is outside the norm; his ability to rationalize his actions becomes important later in the novel.

Literary
Device

As Henry flees from the chaos of war, Crane makes clear that nature is still, and is always, at peace even while its most intelligent creature, man, can be agitated, uncertain, and at war. Indeed, as Henry retreats, he observes the beauty and tranquillity of many dimensions of nature. Nature's peace prevails even amid the noise, disruption, and death, all unnatural behaviors, on the battlefield. This contrast of the tranquility of nature and the agitated actions of man serves to heighten Henry's mental plight.

Glossary

the imbecile line Henry's assessment of his comrades who did not flee.

sagacious things wise decisions (Henry's assessment of his own actions).

Chapter 8

Summary

The sound of a major battle stops Henry's flight. Indeed, it arouses his curiosity, so he makes his way back toward the battle through the forest. He first encounters a field with several dead soldiers. As he hurries past this field, he runs into many wounded men returning from the front lines for medical treatment. He sees several soldiers and one officer. One soldier, "a tattered man, fouled with dust blood, and powder stain from head to shoes," tries to befriend him. The man talks about the bravery shown by the regiment in the battle, but when he asks Henry where he is hit, Henry can't answer him because, of course, he has no wound, and he hurries away from his questioner.

Commentary

For human beings, as well as for nature's other creatures, curiosity may be stronger than fear, and Henry's curiosity gets the better of his fear. The battle sounds are too intriguing to ignore, so Henry reverses his retreat and heads back to the front. Crane writes, "He saw that it was an ironical thing for him to be running thus toward that which he had been at such pains to avoid. But he said, in substance to himself, that if the earth and the moon were about to clash, many persons would doubtless plan to get upon the roofs to witness the collision." This return to the front, then, isn't out of character because Henry's is a very normal reaction for any curious young person.

Stylistically, Crane again uses figurative language in this chapter to make his images of war and of nature come alive. His use of synesthesia (connecting two different senses, for example, color and sound, to create a unique image) is effective as he describes the battle as a "crimson roar." Also, the clarity of the simile used in the line, "The noise was as the voice of an eloquent being," and the nature personification in the line, "Sometimes the brambles formed chains and tried to hold him back," are very effective in developing images in the reader's mind.

Crane comments on the psychology of war as he speculates, through Henry's thoughts, on why soldiers do battle. Henry thinks that there is a false perception that each small battle will be reviewed in print, that heroes and heroic actions will be identified, and that those soldiers who perform heroically will be glorified for their accomplishments. In reality, however, Henry believes that individual accomplishments would appear in print only "under a meek and immaterial title." Nevertheless, Henry concludes that this idealization of battle isn't really bad because he assumes that if the soldiers really knew their insignificance, "in battle every one would surely run." This is Crane's view of war as revealed in Henry's thoughts.

Chapter 9

Summary

Henry returns to walking along with the retreating soldiers. He worries that the soldiers may recognize that he has run from the battle and that they are looking at him and "contemplating the letters of guilt he felt burned into his brow." Indeed, he envies the wounded soldiers and wishes for an emblem of battle, his own "[little] red badge of courage,"—the first reference to the novel's title and a symbol of bravery—rather than having the feelings of guilt which he must keep within. Henry sees "the spectral soldier" stumbling along, waving others away, wanting to be alone. On closer scrutiny, Henry realizes that this dying soldier is Jim Conklin.

Henry is overcome with grief at the sight of Jim's condition. Jim recognizes Henry and tells him that he has only one fear—that he may be run over by a battery coming along the road. He asks Henry to get him out of the road, to keep him safe, if a battery approaches; Henry is so overcome with emotion that he can't answer his friend except with wild gestures. At that point, the tattered soldier overtakes Henry, and the two try to help Jim, but he waves them off. Suddenly, Jim begins to run through the field, followed by Henry and the tattered soldier. Jim stops, and, after several body-shaking convulsions, he stands tall and then dies.

Commentary

Character
Insight

At the beginning of the chapter, Henry possesses a state of reason that allows him to feel guilty about running away. He feels ashamed that he has no wound like the others around him. He longs to carry a symbol of bravery, a wound, indicating that a more normal sense of honor has returned to his mind.

However, Henry seems incapable of acting bravely, even in this less dangerous setting. When Jim asks him to help him get out of the road if a battery comes along, Henry can't muster even the courage to give his friend the assurance that he will help him when the time comes. Henry still exists in a state of conflict between his desire to have courage and his inability to realize these desires in the face of reality. He remains an observer—even as his friend's body falls to the ground, he only stands and watches.

Jim's death is of great significance to Henry primarily because Jim was invincible in Henry's eyes. To see Jim mortally wounded brings Henry face-to-face with his own mortality. As for Jim, his actions appear to be totally consistent with his statements. He stated early on that he would be a team player—that if everybody ran, he would run, and if everybody stood and fought, he would fight. This is what he did, and, in so doing, he has been mortally wounded. As a result, he must find a place to die, so he leaves the road, moves into the field, and dies. This act is the act of a soldier who knows that his time is over, so he must move out of the way. Even though his time as a soldier has ended, the war has not ended, so he moves out of the way to allow the battles to continue.

Because Henry has not been a leader, he has relied on his comrades to be his leaders. When Jim, a true leader for Henry, is wounded and dies, Henry turns inward, a behavior which he has followed throughout the work. Henry does this in an attempt to protect himself psychologically. He does not want his dependence on others to be obvious. This reaction has been a consistent dimension of Henry's character.

The death of Jim isn't totally unexpected by the reader precisely because of the portrayal of this character. Jim's character has been identified as confident, if not overconfident, and the reader anticipates from earlier encounters with Jim that this overconfidence—in this type of war—can't be a good sign. Indeed, Jim's overconfidence foretells something tragic, and this foreshadowing comes to fruition with Jim's death.

This chapter allows the author to highlight, through dialogue, the dialect used by Henry, Jim, and the tattered soldier. Their conversations are battlefield simple, but profoundly sensitive. Crane's extended use of this dialect-filled dialogue helps lend additional realism to this bloody, sad scene, allowing the reader intimate access to the characters and their feelings.

In this chapter, Crane uses a unique combination of oxymoron (a rhetorical figure of speech which combines contradictory terms to form an image) and simile to make an image of the sun: "The sun was pasted in the sky like a [fierce] wafer." This word picture allows Crane, again, to use nature imagery as a contrast to the mundane drudgery of the life of a soldier.

Glossary

a philippic a bitter verbal attack.

Chapter 10

Summary

The tattered soldier's reaction to Jim's death is one of awe. He continues to talk non-stop to Henry and to call Jim a real "jim-dandy." Henry pays little attention to the tattered soldier's ramblings until the soldier, trying to be sympathetic to Henry's supposed wound, says, "Where is your'n located?" Henry tells him angily, "Oh, don't bother me." Indeed, Henry walks away from the tattered soldier, leaving him in the field, even as the tattered soldier shows signs of becoming very disoriented from the effects of his wounds. Henry quickly forgets the tattered soldier and again begins to focus on his own condition, wishing he were dead, noting that the simple question asked by the tattered soldier is representative of a society that will not allow him to "keep his crime concealed in his bosom."

Commentary

Character
Insight

In a key passage in this chapter, Crane tells the reader that Henry "could hear the tattered man bleating plaintively." Henry's reaction to the tattered man's whining is to abandon the disoriented soldier. Ironically, Henry doesn't recognize that he has been the one doing the greatest bleating (if only internally). When he sees that same behavior in another person, he treats that behavior with disdain—unable or unwilling to show compassion or to see that same behavior in himself. Henry has sunk into a state of total self-absorption, the antithesis of the compassion required to be the courageous and honorable man he thinks he wants to be.

After abandoning the tattered soldier in the field, Henry realizes that he is also alone and abandoned. When Henry begins to wish for death, the reader can see that the tattered man's question had pierced his soul. As Crane tells the reader, the question "asserted [represented] a society that probes helplessly at secrets until all is apparent. His late companion's chance persistency made him feel that he could not keep his crime concealed in his bosom." Henry remains selfish, introspective, fearful, and doubtful.

The sequence of emotions outlined in this chapter allows Crane to continue to reinforce both the instability of Henry's mental condition and the themes of duty (specifically, the failure to do one's duty) and doubt—both augmented by Henry's feelings of guilt resulting from his fleeing.

Glossary

jim-dandy a person who is top-notch.

a swad a large number.

little ones the tattered soldier's wounds.

bleating plaintively whining.

Chapter 11

Summary

Soon after leaving the tattered soldier, Henry walks up a small hill which overlooks a road. He sees two groups of soldiers on the road, one in retreat and one heading to the front. As he watches the two groups, he continues thinking about his situation. On the one hand, he feels that the retreating soldiers have vindicated his decision to run. On the other hand, he sees the enthusiasm, purpose, and drive of the advancing soldiers, and this inspires him to think about joining their column.

He begins mentally arguing whether to join the troops, including assessing that he has no rifle and that he won't able to find his regiment. Just as he overcomes those doubts and is about to rejoin the advancing force, a greater doubt grips him. He wonders how he will explain his disappearance to his comrades once he returns to the front, and the more he considers their reactions to any answers that he might give them, the more he realizes that he will be open to great criticism and ridicule. At the conclusion of this internal debate, his courage is depleted, doubt wins out, and his resolve to rejoin the advancing troops is lost.

Commentary

Character
Insight

In this chapter, Crane again focuses on Henry's mental debate. The reader sees Henry's thoughts swing, in just a few pages, from elation to depression. At one moment, Henry fantasizes about how glorious it might be if he were to die in battle. Then, in the next instant, he counts the many reasons why he can't join the battle. The realization that he can't go back to the battle, where he might face ridicule, sends him into a fit of self-loathing—he says of himself, ". . . he was the most unutterably selfish man in existence." These swings in emotion reveal Henry's instability, an instability compounded by the actions which he has taken and by his deteriorating physical condition.

Literary Device

Color plays an important part in describing Henry's mental condition and his environment in this chapter. Henry experiences "the black weight of his woe"; he is both "a blue desperate figure" and "a blue, determined figure"; he fantasizes that he "stood before a crimson and steel assault"; he "soared on the red wings of war"; the army was "a blue machine." All these colors provide a bright contrast to the drab condition of Henry, and they are supportive of the beauty of nature which continues to shine through the death, dirt, and grime of war. Although these colors do not relate to actual images in nature (these colors are associated with the activities of men in war), Crane uses nature to describe actions associated with men. In effect, these colors do not focus so much on nature's beauty, rather on nature's influence on all creation.

It is also interesting to note that it isn't until this chapter that the reader learns Henry's full name—Henry Fleming. The presentation of the full name comes through one of Henry's imagined encounters with his comrades—this time when his comrades connect his name with his running away: "Where's Henry Fleming He run, didn't 'e? Oh, my!" The use of Henry's full name indicates the strength of his fear of being discovered as a runner; there is no place to hide when someone knows your full name.

Glossary

a symmetrical act Henry is trying to justify his running from battle as being no worse than the army's retreat from battle.

heart of the din the front line.

the indefinite cause the unknown force which caused Henry to run.

a cowled man a hooded man.

mothlike quality the force which kept Henry near the battle (the moth is attracted to the flame).

that mighty blue machine the Union Army.

a slang phrase Henry's name, like a slang phrase, would be used derisively. He has become an object of contempt.

Chapter 12

Summary

Henry sees that the advancing soldiers are suddenly streaming out of the woods in full retreat. As they flee, they run straight toward his position, and soon he is surrounded by fearful, disoriented soldiers, determined to move to a safer position. Henry grabs one soldier and attempts to ask him why he is retreating, but the soldier has no intention of talking to Henry, and, when Henry doesn't release him, the soldier strikes him over the head with his rifle. Henry is badly dazed by the blow, and he struggles to stay conscious as he runs with the retreating soldiers.

Henry then hears "a cheery voice," the voice of a soldier who recognizes that Henry is hurting and who helps him walk along. The cheery-voiced soldier's conversation rambles over many topics. During this one-way conversation, the cheery soldier learns that Henry's regiment is the 304th. The two continue walking, they eventually arrive at the campsite of Henry's regiment, and the cheery soldier leaves him.

Commentary

Literary Device

Ironically, the symbolic "red badge" which Henry receives in this chapter isn't a symbol of courage but rather of question, and, what's more, the red badge is delivered, not by an enemy, but by a comrade. Throughout the book, Henry has questioned everything—why he joined, whether he will stand and fight or run, and so on. It is significant to Henry's characterization that his red badge is not the result of contact with a bullet, but of contact with a question.

Another ironic twist results when the cheery-voiced soldier returns Henry to his regiment. The soldier feels that he is removing Henry from danger, but for Henry, who has thought about all the negative ramifications of his returning to his regiment, returning to his regiment actually places him in danger. The fact that Henry is "cheerily" delivered to his regiment is an ironic contrast to the sadness which he assumes must follow his explanation of his whereabouts.

Character Insight

Indeed, "As he [the cheery soldier] who had so befriended him was thus passing out of his [Henry's] life [after returning him to his regiment], it suddenly occurred to the youth that he had not once seen his face." This realization is also important to Henry's characterization; Henry has the opportunity to look into the face of happiness, but he doesn't do so, because he is so engrossed in his own sadness and doubt. He remains totally absorbed in himself—even the unselfish help of the cherry soldier isn't enough to jar Henry out of the conflict in his mind.

In this chapter, Crane uses similar colors to paint both images of war and nature's response to war. As Crane describes the battlefield, he uses words like "blue smoke," "blue haze," and "pink glare," and war is described as a "red animal." As he describes nature, he chooses words like "orange light," "purple shadows and darkness," and "a blue and somber sky." As seen in previous chapters, Crane, again, uses color imagery to focus on nature's influence on both man's environment and man's behavior.

The images of war created by Crane in this chapter make the war, including its setting in nature, its weapons, and its combatants, vividly understandable to the reader. Crane gives the war a body, including a face and a personality.

Glossary

the flaming wings of lightning the vision seen by Henry after he is struck over the head.

a gauntleted hand a gauntlet is a long glove with a flaring cuff covering the lower part of the arm.

cavalry mounted troops.

facings the trimmings, collar, and cuffs of their military coats.

a great ruck of men and munitions a large quantity of soldiers and munitions.

the swash of the fragrant water the splashing of water.

the valor of a gamin the courage (needed for survival) of a street urchin.

a besplashed charger an officer's beautiful, paint horse.

Chapter 13

Summary

As Henry approaches the campfire, he is stopped by a sentry. The sentry is Wilson, who is overjoyed to see Henry because he feared that Henry had been killed in battle. As the two talk, Henry explains his disappearance by saying that he got separated from the company, and he extends this falsehood by saying that he also got shot in the head. The corporal, Simpson, overhears this conversation (the other men, including an officer, are all asleep) and asks Wilson what is going on. Wilson explains that Henry has returned, and Simpson comments that if men continue to return at this rate over the course of the night, by morning, the entire company will be back.

Simpson tells Henry to sit down, and Henry does so with great relief. Wilson comforts Henry, dresses his head wound (commenting on the unusual nature if this head wound—a wound which looked more like someone had hit him over the head rather than a bullet wound), lets him have some coffee, and gives him his blankets for the night.

Commentary

Theme

The themes of doubt and duty are addressed in this chapter as the reader sees the company, as demonstrated through the behavior of Wilson and Simpson, welcome, without question, the return of Henry. In their duties as soldiers and as friends, his comrades care for him, joyfully accepting his return.

Henry, on the other hand, responds to their kindness with doubt and lies. Henry doubts that his comrades can accept that he was overcome by fear and ran from battle, and, what's more, that they would forgive him for this breakdown. Rather than face the possibility of ridicule and scorn, he lies.

Henry makes up a story to cover-up his disappearance and his injury. In describing Henry telling these falsehoods, Crane uses a significant prepositional phrase which further complicates the reader's decision about whether to sympathize with Henry or to think of him as a calculating, selfish young man who does whatever is necessary to cover-up any questions regarding his commitment to duty. When Henry answers Corporal Simpson's question, "Where was yeh?" Crane writes Henry's answer as, "'Over on th' right. I got separated'—began the youth with considerable glibness." The prepositional phrase at issue is "with considerable glibness." (Synonyms for "glib" include "slick," "smooth," and "easy.") Henry doesn't stammer or stutter as he has done in the past when asked a similar question. Indeed, the phrase includes the intensifying adjective, "considerable."

Typically, Henry begins establishing his story with youthful confidence. But later, when his friend discusses his head wound further, Henry's glibness disappears, and he only fumbles with a button on his jacket in response. His initial glibness may disgust the reader and lead to the decision that Henry isn't capable of true honor. His retreat from this glibness is a sign that Henry is ashamed of the lies and his rejection of duty, which shows hope that he can return to valor.

This hope is given additional fuel when Henry shows concern for someone other than himself. After his friend gives Henry his blankets to sleep on, Henry asks where and on what the friend will sleep. It is the first time that Henry shows compassion and a feeling of connection with his fellow soldiers; this compassion and connection may enable Henry to face battle bravely and attain the honor that he craves.

Glossary

the barbed missiles of ridicule hurtful cutting remarks; insults.

a crone stooping an ugly, withered old woman.

Chapter 14

Summary

Henry sleeps soundly. He is awakened by the noise of battle. As he awakens, he sees the forms of men lying around him. Not remembering where he is, he thinks that he is surrounded by corpses and that he is resting among them. He soon remembers where he is, and the sound of the morning bugle calls all these "corpses," including himself, back to life. Wilson, the loud soldier, greets him heartily, but Henry responds angrily—especially as he reacts to his throbbing head injury. Wilson, however, persists in helping Henry, and Henry marvels at how Wilson has changed from a boastful, agitated soldier to a veteran who can show compassion and care for a comrade. When Wilson asks Henry to assess the prospects for winning the next battle on this day, Henry responds as if he were a battle-hardened veteran, commenting on the ferocity of yesterday's battle and the tenacity of the rebel forces. Henry also mentions that Jim Conklin has been killed, and Wilson seems genuinely moved by this news.

While Henry and Wilson are talking, three soldiers get into a heated argument, and Wilson tries to calm them down. Henry is impressed with Wilson's strength of character and his willingness to put himself in jeopardy for the good of others. Henry mentions that he recognizes how much that Wilson has changed. Wilson makes light of Henry's remarks, and the chapter closes when Wilson comments that the regiment's numbers are not as low as he had thought because many men are returning from being separated from the regiment, "Jest like you [Henry] done."

Commentary

Character Insight

In this chapter, Crane shows the reader some interesting reversals in the characters of Henry and Wilson. Wilson, the loud, practical soldier, has become Wilson, the compassionate, caring, veteran soldier. Crane describes the change in Wilson through Henry's thoughts, "Apparently the other (Wilson) had now climbed a peak of wisdom from which he could perceive himself as a very wee thing. And the youth saw that ever after it would be easier to live in his friend's neighborhood."

Henry's reaction to this realization about his friend shows that he too is on the path toward change. Rather than resenting his friend's newfound calm, evidently brought on by confidence gained in battle, or comparing his friend's calm with his own lack of assurance and certitude, Henry simply accepts that his friend has changed, and he seems happy for him. Henry also remembers to tell Wilson about Jim Conklin's death, showing that he is drawing further away from thoughts about himself and closer to connecting to the other men of his regiment. The reader should remember, however, that Henry's peace of mind is built on a lie, which doesn't bode well for his ability to achieve true honor.

Glossary

a heraldic wind of the day a morning breeze which will be the harbinger of the things that will transpire on this day.

a charnel place a place where corpses are deposited.

the soldier's bath the act of yawning and stretching at daybreak.

the rebs rebels, Confederate soldiers.

light-footed soldiers smaller men who are able to move quickly.

Chapter 15

Summary

As the regiment prepares to move out, Henry and Wilson are marching together. Henry realizes that he is still carrying the letters which Wilson had given him when Wilson thought that he was going to die in battle. With this realization, Henry becomes confident, almost swaggering. He decides not to mention the letters to Wilson, and instead rejoices, knowing that the secret of the letters gives him the power to snub any questions that Wilson may ask him about his head wound.

Henry feels superior to his friend, and he begins to rationalize his former behavior. He looks with disdain on the other soldiers who ran because, of course, their running could not compare to his running. His retreat was heroic, while theirs was tragic.

When Wilson asks for his letters back, Henry feels magnanimous in returning them without saying anything derogatory or deprecating. He feels that he is now "an individual of extraordinary virtues," and he looks forward to returning home to tell of the glories of war.

Commentary

Character Insight

Henry's rationalization of his actions and his delusions of grandeur reach their apex in this chapter. When Henry realizes that he still holds Wilson's letters, he is suddenly transformed into a powerful being. He takes his strength from Wilson's weakness. Indeed, in thinking about this packet of letters, Henry's "self pride was entirely restored." Beyond that, he begins to believe that he really has accomplished something great. In his thinking, he builds his case for greatness to the point that "He returned to his old belief in the ultimate, astounding success of his life" and "He saw plainly that he was the chosen of some gods."

The reader may wonder how remembering the letters could bring about such a change in Henry; however, Crane has shown that Henry has had previous mood swings, and his confidence has always been related to his mood rather than to reality.

Crane reveals in this chapter a person who rationalizes his behavior totally, a personality with delusions of grandeur—but with no basis for these delusions—except for the idea that others' weaknesses are greater than his. It becomes doubtful whether Henry can ever achieve true greatness since his only source of confidence comes from delighting in the weakness of others.

This entire chapter is a study in the rationalizing of behavior. Henry has made a monumental shift in his position, a shift from doubt to confidence to duty, a shift which overtly is based upon delusion. The shift appears to have no basis in reality; however, for Henry, fantasy may be reality, and, if this is the case, this shift could be permanent.

Glossary

order arms to bring the rifle to an upright position with its butt on the ground beside the right foot, and remain at attention.

red speeches Henry's angry arguments with nature.

out among the dragons Henry's facing the enemy in battle.

a small weapon Henry's holding of Wilson's letters.

doomed to greatness an oxymoron for Henry's convoluted thinking that the behavior which doomed him may now be his salvation.

they drank his recitals Henry imagines that the two women will be held spellbound by his war stories and will regard him as a hero.

Chapter 16

Summary

Henry's regiment moves toward the front line to relieve a unit which has been engaged in battle. While marching toward the battle line, the men are surrounded by the noise of battle. Henry and Wilson march together. As they march, they hear talk of disasters befalling their comrades, and the troops begin to grumble about their leadership. Henry, whose confidence is soaring, voices his criticism of their situation as he places the blame for the army's losses on their generals. At one point, a soldier walking next to Henry questions his bravery by asking him if he thinks that he fought the whole battle on the previous day. This comment has a chilling effect on Henry because it forces him to think about his retreat on the previous day.

The troops take up their positions and wait. As they wait, they note the enemy's movements, and the troops again become restless. At this point, their company's lieutenant loses his temper after listening to the men's complaints, and the lieutenant's comments silence the soldiers.

Finally, the regiment hears the increasing sounds of rifle fire and the roar of guns, and the battle begins. There is little enthusiasm for what is to come because the men are already worn out and exhausted from previous battles.

Commentary

In this chapter, Crane uses conversation among the soldiers to advance the character development of both Henry and the other soldiers in the regiment. Henry vocalizes his new-found confidence by criticizing the generals who are leading the troops. On two occasions he calls the generals "derned old lunkheads." This is quite a confident statement from one who not so many hours ago had no confidence.

What's more, Henry also talks about the great effort of these troops, and he includes himself in those efforts. He says, "Well, don't we fight like the devil? Don't we do all that men can? The brigadier said he never saw a reg'ment fight the way we fought yestirday, didn't he?" Again, Henry includes himself in this review, and since no one challenges his being a part of the fighting, he presses his point that their lack of success is the fault of their leaders.

At one point in his tirade Henry is challenged by a soldier who suggests that perhaps he fought the whole battle yesterday. This makes Henry revert to his fear mode, but when no one picks up on this challenge, Henry regains his confidence and continues his attack on what he considers to be their poor leadership.

Crane also reasserts his previous characterization of officers as being strong leaders as the reader sees the lieutenant cool Henry's verbal heat. The lieutenant tells the grumbling company, "You boys shut right up! You've been jawin' like a lot a ol' hens. Less talkin' an' more fightin' is what's best for you boys. I never saw sech gabblin' jackasses." Not one soldier challenges the lieutenant (certainly not Henry). The lieutenant is strong; he is in control; he is, without question, a leader. It's easy for Henry to criticize a distant general, but Henry can't criticize his company's leadership because, of course, the company leaders, including the lieutenant, do lead, and both Henry and the men know it.

Theme

Regarding the themes of duty and doubt, if a reader were to begin the novel at this chapter, the reader would assume that Henry is a confident, battle-ready veteran. Indeed, the reader would most certainly identify Henry with the theme of duty, not doubt. Henry's confidence, which stems from his having rationalized his fleeing as being more acceptable than the others who fled from battle, is very high, so high that he even engages in criticizing the general of his army. His confidence has led him to a spirit of duty which has overcome his prevalent attitude of doubt.

Glossary

black looks critical facial expressions.

chin music pointless talking.

Chapter 17

Summary

Henry and his regiment are in a defensive position, awaiting the charge of the enemy. Henry becomes increasingly agitated and angry because the enemy never seems to tire, and his regiment is dog-tired. He peers through the smoke and haze hoping to catch a glimpse of the enemy. All the while, his anger continues to build.

When the charge does come, Henry fires so often that the barrel of his rifle becomes blisteringly hot. He continues to fire until a comrade tells him that he is firing at nothing because the enemy has withdrawn. His lieutenant is overjoyed with his efforts. Indeed, the lieutenant says, "By heavens, if I had ten thousand wild cats like you, I could tear the stomach out of this war in less than a week." Henry is such a fighting machine that his comrades now look upon him as "a war devil."

When Henry realizes that the enemy has disengaged, he drops to the ground exhausted and burning with thirst. The troops see that even though the enemy has lost many men, this respite will be short lived, so they rest in preparation for the next battle.

Commentary

Character Insight

Crane shows a new characterization of Henry in this chapter. Henry realizes that he is, in fact, a soldier and that he must kill or be killed. Henry becomes angry with the idea that the enemy never seems to tire. In Henry's mind, "Those other men seemed never to grow weary; they were fighting with their old speed. He had a wild hate for the relentless foe." Henry is a changed person; he is now a soldier.

In allowing Henry to reflect on what happens in this small battle, Crane further reveals Henry's evolving character. For example, Crane states that "These incidents made the youth ponder. It was revealed to him that he was a barbarian, a beast." What's more, Henry comes to the realization that "By this struggle, he had overcome obstacles which he had admitted to be mountains. They had fallen like paper peaks, and he was now what he called a hero." This is the new Henry, the soldier-hero. The new confidence that was borne of a lie has finally become the truth.

This chapter shifts the reader into a different relationship with Henry. To this point, the reader has seen Henry move between paranoia and schizophrenia. Henry has been a person for whom the reader has had little respect and less sympathy. By the end of this chapter, however, the reader is willing to forgive and to forget all that has happened and to agree that Henry, if not a hero, is certainly a courageous, confident soldier.

Glossary

an engine of annihilating power Henry's rifle.

beams of crimson the flashes of rifle fire.

Chapter 18

Summary

As the battle ends, Henry and Wilson volunteer to go for water. Unfortunately, they can't find the stream, and the two start back to their lines. In the distance, they see a group of officers riding in a hurry. The officers include the commander of their division. As the two infantrymen slowly walk past the officers, they listen to the discussion and hear that the enemy is forming another charge. They hear the general ask the other officers what troops could be spared for launching an offensive against the enemy. When the two infantrymen hear that their regiment has been chosen for the charge, they hurry back to their company with the news. The lieutenant is upset with their dallying, but when they announce that their company is going to charge the enemy, the officer is very excited for the opportunity. Henry and Wilson, however, don't tell the final words which they hear the general say: "I don't believe many of your mule drivers will get back."

The officers begin organizing the troops for the charge. The soldiers realize what they need to do; they are not hesitant. They simply await the command. Just as they are ready to charge, one of the soldiers makes the prophetic statement, "We'll git swallowed."

Commentary

This chapter allows Crane to set the stage for an action which the regiment hasn't yet engaged in—an offensive charge. This offensive is a major event for the 304th, even if it is only one small battle in the larger war.

Henry, on realizing that there will be a charge, comes to the realization that he is really "insignificant." The entire regiment, in the eyes of one of the officers, isn't more than a "broom" needed to sweep out "some part of the woods." For the men of the 304th, however, this is their war, this is their first offensive, and they will do their best. The reader sees that the regiment is blindly willing to do what is considered their duty.

The characterization in this chapter focuses on the officers, who are realists. One of them calls the troops of the 304th "mule drivers," meaning that they are rough-and-tumble troops, not a smooth and polished unit of veterans. At the same time, however, the general of this division recognizes that these men are needed, and he shows both compassion and realism when he says, "Get 'em ready, then. I'll watch developments from here, an' send you word when to start them." As the other officer salutes, the general adds, "I don't believe many of your mule drivers will get back." Crane creates an implication of resolution with a touch of sorrow in this response, but the general must send men into battle knowing that many will die. This is his responsibility, his duty, and this decision must be his, so he makes it.

Crane continues to characterize the officers as strong, motivated, enthusiastic leaders. At the same time, they recognize the courage shown by their troops, and they know that the lives of these men are in their hands.

Glossary

the ragged line the regiment's condition after repelling the enemy's charge.

a jangling general refers to the jangling noise that a general's sword and medals make as he rides on horseback.

Chapter 19

Summary

The charge begins. Henry runs toward a clump of trees, expecting to meet the enemy at that location. As Henry runs, he hears the shouts of the enemy and sees men fall to the ground in agony and death. As the charge continues, the men begin to cheer; however, this pace takes its toll on the soldiers, and the charge begins to slow. The men hesitate.

Suddenly, "the roar of the lieutenant" brings the men back to reality. The lieutenant cajoles and curses the men into action. Finally, Wilson jumps forward and fires a shot into the trees hiding the enemy. This action arouses the other men, and they all commence firing.

Eventually, the regiment reaches a clearing, and the men take up positions behind a row of trees which border the clearing. Again, however, the men appear to lose their resolve. Once more, the lieutenant brings the men back to reality. He shouts directly at Henry when he says, "Come on, yeh lunkhead! Come on! We'll all git killed if we stay here." Henry takes the initiative and begins to run across the field.

The lieutenant and Wilson both join him, and they urge the rest of the men to follow. The men do follow, and as Henry runs, he finds that he is running near the color sergeant who is carrying the flag. Henry feels a great love and pride envelop him as he sees the flag. At that moment, the color sergeant is mortally wounded. As he falls forward, Wilson grabs the flag, and, with Henry's help, they take the flag from the dead soldier whose body falls to the ground.

Commentary

Crane strengthens the reader's belief in the reality of Henry's character change in this chapter. As the chapter begins, Henry responds without hesitation to the signal to charge. Indeed, he charges with such enthusiasm that he is described as "an insane soldier." But Henry isn't alone in his enthusiasm—the other soldiers are also in a "frenzy," "a furious rush." "They possessed a mad enthusiasm that it seemed would be incapable of checking itself before granite and brass." Henry's enthusiasm infects the other troops, and he is, indeed, the leader of the charge (behind the officers, of course).

Henry's struggle between doubt and duty seems to have disappeared. There is no question that duty is the dominant force now motivating Henry. His actions and behaviors throughout the last two chapters have been courageous, indeed heroic. Henry is becoming the personification of the word duty.

Crane consistently shows the officers to be leaders who have the ability and courage to inspire their troops. Crane is consistent in his characterization of the officers as leaders because the officers must be consistent in their leadership with their troops, and they are. The front-line officers do not hesitate to lead their men into battle. The brigade officers do not hesitate to critique the actions of the battlefield officers in carrying out an overall strategy. Crane is emphasizing leadership within the chain of command. The soldiers recognize this, and, although they may not always agree with the strategy selected, they do follow because they have confidence in their leadership, which has now grown to include Henry.

Glossary

the lurid lines the enemy's battle line.

the yellow tongues the smoke and fire emanating from the rifle barrels of the enemy.

incapable of checking itself before granite and brass the enthusiastic charge of the regiment would not be stopped by even the hardest of objects (granite and brass), let alone by enemy soldiers.

Chapter 20

Summary

As quickly as the charge begins and continues, it comes to an end. Henry sees that the remaining troops in the regiment are beginning to retreat. The officers entreat the men to keep firing, but to no avail. The regiment's remaining men return to the relative safety of the trees on the side of the clearing where the offensive began. Henry and Wilson have a brief argument over who will carry the flag. Henry pushes Wilson away and assumes the ownership of the flag. As Henry surveys his comrades, he sees a dejected, worn-out group of soldiers. The enemy forces begin their counterattack against the retreating regiment.

The regiment is in serious disarray, and Henry joins forces with his lieutenant to try to keep the men focused on their retreat toward friendly lines. Confusion builds, and some of the troops in Henry's regiment begin to think that they are moving toward the enemy instead of away from them. Henry moves into the middle of the confused troops, and he, while holding the flag as a rallying point, along with the lieutenant and the other officers, brings the men back to their senses. The lieutenant organizes the troops into a circle in order to cover any possibility that the troops have lost their direction and to protect the remaining men in the regiment from attack from any direction.

As the regiment waits, Henry studies the demeanor of the lieutenant. The lieutenant is calm as he stands straight and peers through the haze—when, suddenly, he hollers, "Here they come! Right on us, b' Gawd!" Henry and the others begin firing. The enemy is so close that Henry can clearly see, for the first time, the faces and uniforms of the enemy. The quick action of the regiment catches the enemy troops by surprise. The enemy returns fire, and the two forces engage in a fierce battle. Henry is impressed with the ferocity the regiment shows in fighting. The remaining soldiers of the regiment turn back the enemy. This "small duel" revitalizes the men and restores their confidence.

Commentary

In this chapter, Crane focuses on the collective regimental confidence. This focus on the regiment as a unit allows Crane to place Henry in the context of both his fighting unit in particular and of war in general. Henry is an infantry man, a foot soldier, no better nor worse than all the others in his unit. This war is not his war. It is a war involving the Henrys, Jims, and Wilsons on both sides of the conflict. Crane expects the reader to place Henry in this context because Henry, in reality, is but one small cog in the gears of war. The confidence of each soldier combines to form a confident unit of soldiers.

This chapter shows clearly how the unit's confidence, as a whole, is dependent on the confidence of individual soldiers. At the same time, Henry's willingness, indeed his eagerness, to be the flag bearer illustrates his courage and recognition of duty. His behavior can be coupled with the brave leadership of the lieutenant in leading the troops into battle and in protecting them when under attack. The actions of these two men help to build the confidence of the unit to the point that they can mount an offensive and eventually repel a counterattack.

Henry works closely with a bold leader, the lieutenant. Henry holds the flag as a rallying point for the regiment. He dismisses a friend who loses his confidence as he tells him, "Oh shut up, you damned fool!" Henry will not listen to whining men with a loser mentality.

Literary Device

Crane develops a strong broom metaphor as he discusses the idea that the regiment is to act as a broom to sweep out the enemy. This metaphor stops when the regiment's offensive stops. It is picked up again when the enemy's counterattack is suggested to swallow the regimental broom. If Henry's regiment (the regimental broom) is, in fact, going to be "swallowed" by the enemy, Henry hopes that, at least, he wants "the consolation of going down with the bristles forward." This metaphor for anger with the enemy, for choking the enemy, works well.

Crane uses the broom metaphor in conjunction with the regiment's offensive because the broom is a well-recognized cleaning tool. At the same time, a broom is not usually considered to be a weapon; however, in this case Crane makes the broom a weapon metaphorically by changing its use from a cleaning tool to a weapon (if used with the bristles forward to choke). In this way, Crane is suggesting metaphorically that the regiment (a common fighting unit) can use common tools (a broom) to achieve a common goal (victory in battle).

The use of smoke, haze, fog, and clouds as symbols for the confusion of war is especially important for this chapter. The battles are fought in smoke, haze, fog, and clouds. The war is unclear; the battles are hazy, even if they do end in victory. The use of these symbols leads the reader to ask, "Where is this all going?"

Glossary

the lurid lines the regiment's view of the enemy's rifles as seen through the haze of the battlefield.

the impetus of enthusiasm the regiment has regained its confidence and enthusiasm for battle.

Chapter 21

Summary

After repelling the enemy counterattack, Henry and the remainder of his regiment return to their lines where they are greeted with taunts and derogatory comments made by another regiment. Henry is angered by the comments, as are the lieutenant and the red-bearded officer. Henry looks back at the distance which the regiment covered in the charge, and he realizes, with surprise, that they really had not ventured very far from their line. He begins to think that the jeers of the greeting regiment are justified. However, as Henry reflects further on the charge, he feels quite happy and contented with his own personal performance during the battle.

As the men are resting, the general who recommended that the 304th lead the charge rides into the camp and confronts the colonel of the regiment and criticizes the efforts of the men. He wants to know why the regiment could not have gone another 100 feet across the lot. The regiment's colonel seems prepared to respond angrily to the critical officer; however, he backs down. The general leaves in a huff. The lieutenant, who overhears the general's remarks, begins to defend the regiment's efforts, but he is rebuffed by the colonel. The other soldiers, including Henry and Wilson, defend their efforts and recount their efforts with praise. The more they talk, the angrier they get with the general.

At this point, however, several soldiers begin to retell a conversation which they overheard between the colonel and the lieutenant. The colonel asked the lieutenant who was carrying the flag during the charge. When the lieutenant tells the colonel that it was Fleming, the colonel calls Henry a "jimhickey," a term of great praise. The lieutenant also tells the colonel that Wilson was at the front of the charge along with Henry. As a result of hearing these comments, both Henry and Wilson feel great pride and contentment with their efforts.

Commentary

Character
Insight

When Henry and the regiment return to their lines after their charge, and after repelling the enemy's counterattack, they are greeted with derision by a waiting regiment. Henry's reaction is one of anger. The reader has seen Henry's anger approach the level of hate on other occasions in recent encounters with the enemy. Now Henry feels hate even for his fellow troops. He is an anger machine which could boil into hate for anything or anyone who challenges his courage or the courage of his regiment. This is quite a change from the fearful, doubting Henry whom the reader saw earlier in the book.

At the same time, Henry is also characterized as a realistic soldier. When he reviews the actions of his regiment in terms of the territory covered in the charge, he realizes that the distances covered "were trivial and ridiculous." He considers that perhaps the criticism of his regiment by the other regiment is justified. When he sees his disheveled regiment "gulping at their canteens," he feels disgust for their weakness because he thinks of his own behavior and performance during the charge and is quite pleased.

Theme

Thematically, this chapter continues to focus on duty and confidence. Henry knows that he has performed well. His commanding officer has praised him as a "jimhickey" soldier. He is initially angered by the criticism of the other regiment, but, on reflection, he can see their point. This shows maturity and confidence in his ability. As Henry's confidence grows, and as he learns the concept of duty, he is becoming an outstanding soldier.

Style &
Language

The dialogue between the soldiers recorded at the end of the chapter makes extensive use of dialect. For example, one soldier says, "Well, sir, th' colonel met your lieutenant right by us—it was the damndest thing I ever heard—an' he ses: 'Ahem! Ahem!' he ses. 'Mr. Hasbrouck!' he ses, by the way, who was that lad what carried the flag?' he ses, . . ." This use of dialect allows the reader to see that soldiers are men, not machines. The soldiers have the same need for information, for praise, and for recognition, as well as the need to use the language which they know (their dialect) to share these needs with others—as do all human beings.

Finally, a tone of foreboding overshadows this chapter. There is an unsettling feeling that perhaps things are going too well psychologically and behaviorally for Henry. This is war, and war is unpredictable. The reader senses that Henry's newfound confidence and enthusiastic acceptance of duty are very fragile. They might shatter if, for example, something were to happen to the lieutenant, to Wilson, to Henry himself, or to another soldier who is close to Henry.

Glossary

dusty blue lines other Union regiments returning to their lines after participating in battles.

the depleted band the condition of Henry's regiment on returning from the offensive.

ragamuffin interest the soldiers' uniforms were tattered and torn (a ragamuffin appearance), yet the soldiers still had a keen interest in overhearing the conversation between the colonel and the general.

black words between officers the possible verbal confrontation between the general and the colonel is of great interest to the listening regiment.

the colonel's manner changed from that of a deacon to that of a Frenchman the colonel's initial response to the general's criticism of the regiment's efforts was "to defend with vigor" (a deacon's response) the regiment's actions; instead he chooses "to respond diplomatically" (a Frenchman's response).

elfin thoughts of or like an elf; here, meaning that Henry realizes on his return to his lines that the regiment really had not accomplished very much. What they had done they had exaggerated (fantasized—"elfin, fairy-like") into something more than what was actually accomplished.

Chapter 22

Summary

After resting briefly from the last battle, Henry watches the battle lines reform. Then Henry's regiment is called into action. The men respond enthusiastically, at first, as they return the fire of the enemy, but soon the incessant whiz of bullets from undiminishing Rebel rifle fire leaves them more discouraged and besmirched than after their last battle. The lieutenant tries to prod his troops to move forward, but they don't move. Henry continues his role as flag bearer, and, as such, as an observer of all that is happening.

Suddenly, the regiment sees the enemy troops charging so rapidly and at so close a range that they can see the excitement of the charge in the faces of the enemy. Without waiting for an order, the 304th fires a "flock of bullets" in one great volley. This stops the charge as the opposing troops take cover behind a fence line. They immediately return fire and, because of their protected position, do considerable damage.

However, the regiment continues to fight with enthusiasm. Henry is impressed with the bravery of his comrades, so impressed that he decides that his final act of revenge on the officer who called the 304th "mule drivers" and "mud diggers" would be to die upon this field. As the chapter ends, Henry realizes that the regiment is losing its resolve to fight.

Commentary

Theme

The themes of duty and honor come to the fore in this chapter. The men are tired, hungry, and thirsty, yet when their unit is called up to do battle, Crane tells the reader that "the emaciated regiment bustled forth with undiminished fierceness." The troops, on both sides, achieve honor by their continued willingness to do battle even when objectives are unclear, supplies are low, wounds are matter-of-fact, and death, whether painfully slow or mercifully quick, is a reality for each soldier in the battle. Duty and honor are the products of courage. The troops fighting in this war on both sides show unbelievable courage.

Henry initially embraced the Greek ideal of dying in battle as a part of his romantic view of war—as seen in his talk with his mother about enlisting. However, as he experiences war, he matures. The romanticizing Henry transforms into a realistic Henry—first as he overcomes his fear in his first battle, then as he runs from his second battle, next, as he leads a charge against the enemy, and finally, as flag bearer, as he watches his comrades dying, and he wishes to honor them and, at the same time, to gain revenge on the name-calling general by leaving "his dead body lying, torn and gluttering, upon the field."

Character
Insight

Henry's wish is one of a veteran soldier, a wish that has moved Henry beyond his selfish, romantic view of dying in battle for personal glory to an understanding that death, whether in support of a cause or in support of comrades, isn't to be feared, but, in fact, is to be accepted—as an act of love. This shows a mature Henry, a selfless, veteran who is a product of war experiences which have moved him to a level of maturity well beyond his chronological age. Henry is no longer a selfish, fearful rookie; he is now a confident, veteran team player.

Glossary

the dark-hued masses/the lighter hued regiments   the Confederate troops.

the dark blue lines/the blue curve   the Union troops.

emaciated regiment/grunting bundles of blue/the robust voice . . . growing rapidly weak   the current status of the 304th regiment (Henry's regiment).

a congregation of horses   a string of horses tied up.

Chapter 23

Summary

As the battle continues, it becomes clear to the officers of Henry's regiment that the troops can't stay in their present position. The officers decide to charge the enemy's position. The objective is to push the enemy away from the fence behind which they are hiding and firing. As quickly as the tired and dispirited regiment hears the command to charge, they respond with renewed strength and zeal. The charge is so successful that the enemy abandons its position, Wilson captures the enemy's flag, and four enemy troops are taken prisoner.

As the celebration of this successful charge of the regiment winds down, Henry sits down in some tall grass and leans his flag against the fence. Wilson, his friend, joins him in resting on the ground.

Commentary

Literary Device

This chapter places the reader in Henry's mind as the decision to charge and the results of that decision unfold. Through Henry's eyes, the reader becomes a combatant. As the charge unfolds, the reader feels Henry's exhilaration and excitement as he and his comrades successfully complete their task. The reader experiences all the emotions, including reactions to suffering and death, associated with but one charge in this bloody war.

The men of Henry's regiment are in the full frenzy of battle, so much so that they seem to be propelled by a force outside themselves—the force of combined commitment to task and duty. Their charge, in the face of an apparently impossible task, is the ultimate act of bravery.

Henry has but one goal, the symbolic act of capturing the opposing regiment's flag. He seeks the flag not for personal glory, but because, "He was capable of profound sacrifices, a tremendous death." When the flag is captured, not by Henry, but with Henry's help, the reader sees that Henry is truly a hero.

Chapter 23 also gives the reader an intimate look at the enemy. Previously in the novel, the enemy is largely characterized as a monstrous, inhuman force. However, in this chapter, the reader sees, through Henry's eyes, the death of the Rebel flag bearer, a death struggle that is just as human as any that has been described in the book for a Union soldier. The reactions of the captured Rebel soldiers are also quite human—diverse and realistic. Clearly, Crane wants the reader to see that the dehumanization necessary to kill another human being is false and wrong. This realization makes the bloodshed on both sides of the conflict that much more tragic. At the same time, however, Crane clearly makes the point that a soldier must recognize his duty, even if this duty requires that he kill or be killed.

Glossary

its faded and jaded condition the condition of the regiment prior to its charging the fence behind which the enemy is hiding.

the iron gates of the impossible the effect on the regiment of the decision to charge the enemy even though the troops are exhausted.

the bleach of death Henry's view of the face of the Confederate color bearer just as he is mortally wounded.

Chapter 24

Summary

As Henry and Wilson rest, they see a large number of troop movements and changes in artillery positions. These movements and changes are not occurring in a rapid, hurried fashion by men preparing for battle, but, rather, in a slower, more leisurely fashion by men beginning to withdraw.

The officers begin to organize the troops for a return to their previous position. The regiment links up with the other regiments in the brigade, as well as with a mass of other troops, and the entire division moves away from the front. The importance of these linkages and this massive movement prompts Henry to say to Wilson, "Well, it's all over." Wilson's reply, "B'Gawd, it is," sends Henry into a detailed, introspective assessment of his entire war experience to this point.

It then begins to rain. As Henry walks in this rain shower, he realizes that "he had rid himself of the red sickness of battle. The sultry nightmare was in the past." As he continues on the road back to his camp, he looks to the sky, and he feels "an existence of soft and eternal peace"—just as the sun breaks through the clouds.

Commentary

In this last chapter, Henry mentally reviews the three significant stages of his battlefield experience. Regarding his second battle and his subsequent flight from the front, Henry attributes that behavior to nothing more than "the wild mistakes and ravings of a novice who didn't comprehend." Indeed that is probably a fair assessment since he was not the first soldier to run, nor would he be the last, and he did recover his courage to make a fine impression on his lieutenant at the next battle. Indeed his captain identified him as a fierce "wild cat". Also, then, when he led the troops as flag bearer, he was very courageous and, rightly so, because he stared into the face of the enemy and didn't back down. Henry's actions show great courage.

The only behavior which truly rests negatively on him—which truly places a heavy feeling of guilt on him—is his treatment of the tattered soldier. When both are in the field, and the tattered soldier, wounded and disoriented, seeks to help Jim, Henry loses patience with him and leaves him. This "vision of cruelty," this "somber phantom of the desertion in the field," this recognition that "the light of his soul flickered with shame" troubles Henry greatly; however, he is able to rationalize this behavior because he decides to use this "sin" as a future force to control his "egotism," as a way to be sure that he remains always humble. He reasons that if he ever begins to feel that his courage exceeds all others, he need only remember that he didn't treat a wounded companion with decency, and that memory will work to bring back his humility. Indeed, for him to reason this way, he must truly be a "man," both of and in war, because he will face future battles, and, as the reader has seen, he has shown the courage and bravery needed to face the enemy squarely.

Henry's comments both about his bravery and courage and about his humility are not idle chatter. Henry has the right and the privilege to "talk the talk" because he has "walked the walk" militarily, so the reader must believe that the "sin" of deserting the tattered soldier will help him control his tendency now to be the most courageous and bravest "man" in the regiment. Indeed, his actions since that incident have proven him to be just that.

Literary Device

Crane concludes this chapter, and this novel, with a series of color images to support the various stages of thinking that Henry experiences on the walk back to the camp. Crane paints these vivid images to reinforce both Henry's thoughts and battles, as well as the environment, both mental and physical, which now live in the mind of the reader.

Symbolically, the red badge of courage is the red badge which brought Henry courage. Only after Henry is hit over the head during his flight from the front is he able to clarify his understanding of his role of what it means to be a soldier, to return to his regiment, and to then become one of the bravest soldiers—if not the bravest, most courageous soldier—in the regiment.

Glossary

the dilapidated regiment Henry's regiment after the assault on the fence line.

the clogged clouds Henry's mental confusion as he reviews his behavior in combat.

the gilded images of memory Henry's thoughts as he thinks of his heroic deeds in battle.

the machinery of the universe nature's plan for the destiny of all creatures.

the bludgeon of correction Henry's guilt regarding his treatment of the tattered man and the actions he needs to take to alleviate that guilt.

the sultry nightmare Henry 's overcoming of all his doubts and short-comings in his transformation into a brave, courageous soldier.

a bedraggled train the last image which the reader gets of Henry's Union division as it returns from all the battles in which it has participated.

CHARACTER ANALYSES

Henry Fleming, a Union Soldier

This novel documents Henry's growth and maturity as a soldier through the changes in his personality and behavior. During this transition, Henry's emotions run the gamut from glory to fear to depression to anger to exhilaration to courage to honor. His personality and behavior move from innocence to experience, in essence from doubt to duty.

Henry's maturing process occurs very quickly. In the span of just a few days, Henry experiences a lifetime's worth of growth—from his enlisting for self-centered reasons of glory, to the exhilaration of his first battle, to his running from his second battle for fear of being killed, and, ultimately, to his facing the enemy and leading a charge as he becomes one of the bravest soldiers in his regiment. Several examples from the novel illuminate the changes which take place in Henry's character.

Henry's confidence, a confidence somewhat related to an under-standing of duty, but also based on the curiosity of youth, is addressed early in the novel. Henry is confident that war will bring him untold glory. Henry's confidence is not shaken by his mother's "impregnable" concerns, so he proceeds with his plan to enlist despite her wishes.

In Chapter 2, however, the focus of Henry's character development moves quickly to Henry's doubts and fears as the regiment moves closer to battle. His thoughts jump from longing for home to conjuring up monster images to describe common occurrences. Fear almost consumes Henry. Henry's doubts continue as he reacts to his environment—both the land and the people. At one point, his fears become so great that "he had concluded that it would be better to get killed directly and end his troubles."

When Henry and his comrades do finally engage in battle, Henry faces the enemy and fires repeatedly, and, eventually, the enemy charge is repelled. Henry finally overcomes a portion of his fears and gains con-fidence as he works with the other soldiers of his regiment to hold the line. With the help of his fellow soldiers, Henry stands his ground and makes some movements toward confidence and maturity.

Henry's newfound confidence is short-lived. The realities of battle intervene and cause his fear and doubt to resurface. Henry moves from a state of euphoria after repelling the enemy's charge in the first battle to a state of panic at the beginning of a second battle. When the enemy charges, Henry's fears take control. When the soldier next to him drops his rifle and runs, Henry's ability to reason vanishes, and he runs. He abandons any thoughts of honor and duty and sinks into a state of total self-concern and immaturity. In his state of disgrace, he attempts to rationalize his retreat to make himself feel better.

Henry remains in this state of self-absorption through some critical events in the novel: Even Jim Conklin's death can't jar him out of his thoughts about his own well-being. He also abandons the tattered soldier because he fears the man's questions about his head wound; he commits a despicably selfish act rather than face his own lack of courage. In fact, his self-absorption is so deep that it stops him from rejoining the fighting, even though he wants to.

Henry's accidental head wound is not the red badge of courage that he longs to acquire; rather, it becomes a shield that he uses to protect the lies he has built around himself. Henry only begins to emerge from his shell of self-absorption and fear when he recognizes Wilson's weakness in giving him a bunch of letters to hold. On this strange foundation, Henry's confidence for battle begins to take shape.

Henry's new-found confidence allows him to face a tough reality: that as a soldier, he must kill or be killed. His confidence allows him to feel anger toward the enemy, rather than fear. At this point, Henry, if not a hero, is certainly a courageous, confident soldier. His confidence gains such strength that it begins to influence the other soldiers. When Henry assumes the role of flag-bearer for the regiment, he becomes a symbol of bravery and courage. His transformation from child to man, from cowardly enlistee to brave veteran, is complete.

The Soldiers

By focusing on selected characters, Crane attempts to portray the various types of soldiers and reactions to battle that can be found in any regiment of any war.

Henry Fleming

Henry represents the young soldier who initially views war as an adventure, as an opportunity for glory. That view changes quickly—as quickly as Henry's first combat experience from which he ends up running. The rest of the novel is the story of the rebuilding of Henry's shattered confidence, his recognizing the reality of war, his overcoming his doubts, and his realizing and embracing his duty as a soldier.

Jim Conklin

Jim Conklin, the tall soldier, represents the confident, realistic, experienced soldier. Jim has enough confidence to be humorous and carefree, and his confidence buoys up the younger, inexperienced soldiers. Jim is the kind of soldier who Henry, and any young soldier, hopes to be. Jim is the soldier who shows no fear, who finds a way to inject humor into battlefield situations. He is the soldier who can keep everyone else relaxed. As a result, when Jim is mortally wounded, his death weakens the confidence of all his comrades because they reason that if Jim, the wise, veteran soldier, can be killed, then certainly that same fate awaits every other soldier—most with far less confidence and savvy than has Jim Conklin.

Wilson

Wilson represents, initially, the pragmatic, if not somewhat boastful, soldier prior to his being in combat. He is the I'll-do-my-job-and-you-do-yours type of soldier. However, after being in combat, his attitude changes; he recognizes his own mortality (as do all soldiers after being in combat), and he becomes more compassionate and caring in his treatment of his comrades.

The tattered soldier

The tattered soldier represents the soldier who talks too much, who asks too many questions. The tattered soldier tries to be everybody's buddy, but, ironically, ends up being alone.

The cheery soldier

The cheery soldier represents most soldiers in most wars. He is compassionate while practical. He knows his way around the battlefield. He knows what questions to ask and what questions not to ask. He leads with quiet confidence and keeps everyone focused.

The Officers

The officers of the 304th New York Regiment, including the lieutenant (Lt. Hasbrouck), the red-bearded officer, the captain, the regimental colonel (Col. MacChesnay), the brigadier general, and the division general, are consistently shown as leaders who demonstrate great courage, sound judgment, and motivation.

In every battle, the officers cajole and encourage their men to fight and to fight harder. Even if the soldiers do not always appreciate the way the officers must treat them in order to motivate them, the treatment is fair and consistent, even if sometimes harsh.

In all instances, the Union officers lead their troops with bravery and courage. The officers give and receive the respect necessary to win battles and, ultimately, to win wars. This is not easy work (to force men to face death—indeed, to lead them into the face of death), but the officers throughout this work do so. Not with malice, but with realistic explanations and motivated language, tempered with an undertone of compassion. They epitomize commitment to duty and honor, the central theme of the novel.

CRITICAL
ESSAYS

The Structure of the Novel

The novel is organized into many short chapters, which creates the impression that the reader is looking at a series of snapshots in a photo album. This technique works most effectively in the chapters which relate to battlefield action; the short chapters highlight the interactions between the soldiers and their environment. The short chapters allow the reader to enter Henry's mind and become part of Henry's mental debate.

In Chapter 1 of *The Red Badge of Courage*, Henry is totally immersed in his own thoughts. As he waits for war, he daydreams about his home, his farm, and the conversation he had had with his mother. By staging the first chapter of the book almost exclusively in Henry's thoughts, Crane sets the stage for Henry's mental transition throughout the book. His initial mental state is one of excitement and unrealistic thoughts of glory. Henry is a dreamer; boys dream; a youth does not think of death—especially the possibility of his own death.

In Chapter 2, Henry begins to interact with the other soldiers in the regiment. Crane shows Henry listening to his comrades discussing the enemy and the battles to come. Henry, the inexperienced youth, can't judge how much truth is in the veterans' tales. This lack of knowledge contributes to his fear, which he internalizes completely, leaving him isolated from the other men. Henry's isolation allows Crane to focus on Henry's mental transition throughout the book; rarely does the story diverge from Henry's thoughts or actions.

In Chapters 3 and 4, Crane uses rumors to play on Henry's fears and doubts. To this point, Henry has observed battles, but his regiment has not yet been in a battle. Fear—in this case, fear of the unknown—grows because Henry has not yet seen the enemy. (The reader experiences the war through Henry's eyes, so the reader easily identifies with Henry's fear of the unknown, unseen enemy.) Indeed, the fear of the unknown is greater than the fear of facing the problem directly. This fear of the unknown is a normal human behavior, one with which all people can identify, and, as a result, the reader can empathize with Henry.

Chapter 5 brings the first real shift in Henry's character. It is the first day of the first battle for Henry and his regiment. Henry stands his ground and fires, forgetting his fears and doubts about his performance. The reader wonders if Henry has crossed the line from youth to man as a result of his first battle. The answer to this question comes in

Chapter 6, when Henry experiences another character shift. In Chapter 6, the enemy troops immediately regroup to begin another charge. This move surprises the Union troops, including Henry, and his fears return. Indeed, he becomes so afraid that he drops his rifle and runs as the enemy approaches. Henry, as a result, returns to being a boy. Crane uses the quick shifts in Henry's character from chapter to chapter to show Henry's unstable mental condition; his courage and commitment to duty don't come from within, but are entirely influenced by external forces which whip him from one extreme to the other.

Henry remains a frightened boy as he continues to run and to try to determine if, when, and how he should return to his regiment to face the ridicule which he thinks that he will surely receive. In Chapter 12, a cheery soldier befriends him and returns him to his regiment. Prior to meeting the cheery soldier, Henry received a head injury inflicted on him by another fleeing soldier, and he left another comrade, a wounded, tattered soldier, wandering in a field because this soldier asked too many questions about him—questions which he refused to answer at that time. Henry's behavior continues to be boyish and immature.

The fact that Henry, ironically, sustained a head wound from another soldier also running from the front line is known only to Henry and to the reader. In this way Crane brings the reader into Henry's mind and allows the reader to speculate regarding just how Henry will explain what has happened to him. The omniscient point of view used by Crane comes into play as Crane tells the reader how the other soldiers react to the wound—the reader and Henry being the only observers having knowledge of how he sustained the injury. Recovery from the head injury buys Henry a little time to consider if he can tell what really happened to him. He determines that he cannot face the ridicule which he might receive if he told the truth, so he does not tell what really happened. (He tells two untruths instead.) It is not until the head wound heals, and he finds Wilson's letters, that he can begin to rebuild his confidence.

On being returned to his regiment, Henry is welcomed by Wilson, a soldier friend, and given treatment for his injury. In this way, Crane shows that Henry is not totally isolated; his fellow soldiers are prepared to accept him as an important and valued member of their team. Henry, however, can't face Wilson to answer any questions because he is ashamed of what he has done. Henry sleeps that night as a boy waiting to be scolded—and forgiven, if possible.

The next morning, in Chapters 14 and 15, the day after he runs from the enemy, Henry realizes that he may not be the worst soldier in the regiment. Wilson asks him to return several letters which he had given to him. (The letters were given to Henry by Wilson because Wilson thought that he was going to die in battle.) Henry realizes that Wilson could also show weakness and fear (in this case even before the regiment had engaged in battle). As a result, Henry regains some of his lost confidence. Henry's reaction to Wilson's letters—building strength on someone else's weakness—may show some immaturity on Henry's part, but it does move him from boy to youth because he is, at least, trying to find something to reestablish his confidence.

From this point on in the novel, the second day of Henry's combat experience, he develops rapidly into a man, into a courageous duty-bound soldier. Indeed, he reaches his full, soldierly manhood in Chapter 17 when he participates in a battle and fights like a "wild cat." Crane shows Henry's transition as he awakens to the realization that he is, in fact, a soldier who must kill. This is Henry, the new Henry, the soldier hero. Henry is a changed person; he is now a soldier and a man.

In the remainder of the novel, Chapters 19 to 24, Henry becomes a model soldier, showing courage and bravery and allegiance to duty. Henry also determines that he will use his poor treatment of the tattered soldier as a reminder that he must balance humility with confidence, a sentiment that marks Henry as a mature person.

Crane structures the novel to show Henry's quick growth from boy to man by the evening of the second day of combat. Crane speaks to a universal truth about war: that boys must quickly become men in order to survive.

The Use of Figurative Language

Stephen Crane consistently uses figurative language to create images that vividly describe all aspects of war. For example, in the passage, "The cold passed reluctantly from the earth, and the retiring fogs revealed an army stretched out on the hills, resting," an example of personification, the cold, the fog, and the army are described as persons with specific behaviors, feelings, and needs. In addition, Crane uses personification to create a personality for the combatants, both collectively and individually. The clauses, "brigades grinned" and "regiments laughed," are good examples. When Henry's voice is described "as bitter as dregs," this simile allows the reader to experience the voice of an individual soldier.

The imagery developed for an impending battle uses similar techniques. The battle is "the blaze" and "a monster"; the combatants are "serpents crawling from hill to hill"; Henry's regiment is a "blasting host" (a killing machine); "red eyes" (enemy campfires) watch across rivers. All these images contribute to an ominous mood of foreboding.

The regiment is sometimes identified as a person, sometimes a monster, and sometimes a reptile. These images cause the reader to lose sight of the fact that the regiment is really a unit of men—of individual soldiers. The continued use of personification draws the reader to a feeling that a battle is a battle of regimental monsters, not of individual men.

In Chapter 5, Crane continues the use of figurative language, including simile, personification, and metaphor, to paint images of war. For example, he writes that "A shell screaming like a storm banshee went over the huddled heads of the reserves," a simile, and "They could see a flag that tossed in the smoke angrily," a personification, and that "The composite monster which had caused the other troops to flee had not then appeared" a metaphor. The enemy is still not visible. The wait for that "composite monster," continues. Just as the troops experience the dreadful wait, the reader feels the same emotions that all the soldiers are feeling. Crane develops this fear by using figurative language to create monster imagery.

Crane employs similes and personification to draw pictures of soldiers and their weapons. For example, a soldier's "eyeballs were about to crack like hot stones"; "The man at the youth's elbow was babbling something soft and tender like the monologue of a babe"; "The guns squatted in a row like savage chiefs." Crane uses both personification and simile in the line, "The cannon with their noses poked slantingly at the ground grunted and grumbled like stout men, brave but with objections to hurry." This line makes the weapons appear to be living creatures. The use of personification in the line, "The sore joints of the regiment creaked as it painfully floundered into position," turns the regiment into one large, tired soldier. Crane's similes describe groups and individuals in these examples: the rebel forces were "running like pursued imps" and Henry, at first, "ran like a rabbit" and, later, "like a blind man."

Crane develops imagery, using metaphor and personification, to make it clear that Henry has lost all his rational powers and that he is in a total state of panic. For example, to Henry, the enemy soldiers are metaphorically "machines of steel," "redoubtable dragons," and "a red and green monster"; the men who were nearest the battle would make the "initial morsels for the dragons"; "the shells flying past him have rows of cruel teeth that grinned at him." These images clearly show Henry's fright of the enemy.

In Chapter 9, Crane continues to use figurative language to support the war motif. He turns machines of war into people by using personification in the line "a crying mass of wagons." He changes Henry by using a simile, "His [Henry's] face would be hidden like the face of a cowled man." Henry (in his own mind) is a "worm" and "a slang phrase." Crane also paints a picture of the battlefield using metaphoric description of battlefield action, examples being, "the heart of the din" (the battle) and "the mighty blue machine" (the Union Army).

In Chapter 11, Crane uses metaphoric language to describe both the enemy and war in several ways, including "The steel fibers had been washed from their hearts," the enemy is the "dragon," "They [the enemy] charged down upon him [Henry] like terrified buffaloes," and war is "the red animal, the blood-swollen god."

In describing the exhaustion of both Henry and the other soldiers, Crane uses a series of similes, including "Henry remained on the ground like a parcel, "and the men were so tired that they appeared "like men drunk with wine." In addition, when Henry finally lies down, he is so tired that Crane describes the action as "The youth got down like a crone stooping," and when the soldiers do sleep, they sleep under a night sky, a sky with "a handful of stars lying, like glittering pebbles, on the black level of the night."

In Chapter 14, Crane's use of simile to describe the sounds of war is very effective. Examples include, "This din of musketry, growing like a released genie of sound, expressed and emphasized the army' plight." His use of personification to describe the batteries' need to breathe, as seen in the line, "The guns were roaring without an instant's pause for breath," leaves the reader longing to take a breath.

In Chapters 12, 13, 14, and 22, Crane includes several more instances of figurative language to describe the enemy, Henry, himself, the weapons of war, the officers, the troops, the battlefield, and the flag. The enemy becomes "a hound taking a mouthful of prisoners." Henry is described in two similes as not "going to be badgered like a kitten chased by boys" and "When the enemy seemed falling back before him and his fellows, he went instantly forward like a dog." Regarding weapons of war, examples of figurative language include Henry's "[rifle] was an engine of annihilating power," "his [Henry's] rifle was [also] an impotent stick," and "the voices of the cannon were mingled in a long and interminable row."

To describe the officers' actions in preparing the soldiers for an offensive, Crane uses a simile to make an understandable comparison: "[The officers] were like critical shepherds struggling with sheep." Crane describes the regiment while resting as, "The regiment snorted and blew." (This is what horses do after running. The horse metaphor works very well for a regiment that has just run across a battlefield.) The regiment is also described as being "the dejected remnant," "the depleted regiment," "a machine run down." These images provide a picture of a tired group of men.

Crane, through Henry, identifies the flag metaphorically in the following manner, "It was a goddess. . . . It was a woman, red and white, hating and loving, that called him with the voice of his hopes" (examples of metaphor and personification).

Crane also combines a simile with the use of personification to describe Henry's run across a battlefield: "The youth ran like a madman to reach the woods before a bullet could discover him." This sentence combines a clear simile ("like a madman") with a personification of the bullet—the bullet tries to "discover" Henry, discovery being a very human endeavor.

The use of personification in describing the smoke as "lazy and ignorant" helps the reader to feel the frustration of the troops. The use of smoke, haze, fog, and clouds as symbols for the confusion of war, for the atmosphere surrounding war, are constant throughout the novel.

At the same time that Crane describes the ugliness of war metaphorically, Crane also uses descriptive vocabulary words and figures of speech to highlight the beauty of nature in the midst of death and destruction. The reader should note the use of a flower metaphor in the image, "the shells looked to be strange war flowers bursting into fierce bloom."

The reader sees repeated use of images of nature, particularly color images, to make the various settings in the novel more vivid. Examples include, "The clouds were tinged an earthlike yellow in the sunrays and in the shadow were a sorry blue" and the flag was "sun-touched." Crane also uses clouds as a symbol for the confusion produced by war.

In Chapters 11 through 13, Crane creates graphic images by combining colors with concepts, settings, attitudes, and individuals. For example, Henry experiences "the black weight of his woe"; he is both "a blue desperate figure" and "a blue, determined figure"; he fantasizes that he "stood before a crimson and steel assault"; he "soared on the red wings of war"; the army was "a blue machine." Battlefield examples include "blue smoke," "blue haze," and "pink glare," and war is described as a "red animal." Evening is described in terms of "orange light," "purple shadows and darkness," and "a blue and somber sky."

Crane's color imagery creates significant contrasts between dark and light, death and life, and drab and colorful. For example, the faces of the sleeping men are "pallid and ghostly"; Henry confronts a "black and monstrous figure"; the campfires gleam of "rose and orange light"; the leaves of the trees were "shifting hues of silver with red"; and "the stars [are] lying, like glittering pebbles, on the black level of the night".

In Chapters 17 through 19 Crane makes use of color imagery to bring the battle alive visually. The rifles being fired released "beams of crimson fire," and "the blue smoke-swallowed line curled and writhed like a snake stepped upon". The reader also sees the regiment face "yellow flames" and "yellow tongues" (rifle fire), "crimson fury" (cannon fire), and "a blue haze of curses" (the lieutenant's exhorting his troops to cross the clearing).

In Chapters 18 and 20, Crane also uses color to create moods and to reveal attitudes. For example, "There was a row of guns making gray clouds . . . filled with large flashes of orange-colored flame." This is a beautiful, but sinister, image that leaves the reader anxious. Equally sinister is the description of a burning house, set afire by a cannon barrage. The burning house is described as "glowing a deep murder red." A "murder red" can be nothing less than a blood red. In creating this red imagery for a burning house, burning as the result of battle in war, Crane reveals his strong feelings about war.

Color imagery also supports a somber mood in Chapter 20 as Crane uses dark and fog imagery to describe the men as they continue their retreat, their "black journey." As they retreat, they are pursued by "a brown mass of troops," troops whom the regiment now fires at through "a rolling gray cloud."

In Chapter 22, Crane uses color imagery and figurative language when describing the battles and the combatants. This helps the reader to identify the combatants, both physically and emotionally. The Union forces are described as "dark-blue lines," "a blue curve," and "a magnificent brigade." Henry's regiment is "the emaciated regiment," "the blue men," "grunting bundles of blue," and "the robust voice . . . growing rapidly weak." Crane's combination of descriptive phrases and figurative language shows the deteriorating status of the regiment. Even the lieutenant is down to "his last box of oaths." This also shows a regiment in desperate straights. At the same time, Crane's describing the rebel forces as "dark-hued masses" and as "hounds taking a mouthful of prisoners" paints a picture of an ominous enemy.

Crane concludes the novel with a series of color images to support the various stages of thinking that Henry experienced on the walk back to the camp. Henry had been "where there was red of blood" and "black of passion," a vivid contrast. Henry's exploits in battle are now etched in his memory as "gilded images" in "purple" and "gold." (These colors are colors of kings.) At the end of this chapter, as the rain begins, Henry walks through "a trough of liquid brown mud," and he rids "himself of the red sickness of battle." Crane employs these images to make Henry's thoughts more vivid—thoughts of battles and the environment that successfully engage the imagination of the reader.

CliffsNotes Review

Use this CliffsNotes Review to test your understanding of the original text, and reinforce what you've learned in this book. After you work through the review and essay questions, identify the quote section, and the fun and useful practice projects, you're well on your way to understanding a comprehensive and meaningful interpretation of Crane's *The Red Badge of Courage*.

Q&A

1. Henry's transformation from being a doubting, worried enlistee to becoming a courageous, brave soldier actually is the result of his combat experiences which occur over what period of time in the novel?

   a. Two days

   b. Several weeks

   c. Twenty-four hours

   d. One year

   e. One month

2. What are the settings for the opening and closing scenes of the novel?

   a. Washington, D.C.

   b. Henry's mother's farm

   c. A road

   d. A campsite

   e. A battlefield

3. Which adjective does not describe all of the officers in the novel?

   a. Dependable

   b. Determined

   c. Deliberate

   d. Decisive

   e. Defeatist

4. Identify the two most significant factors which helped Henry change his attitude from being overwhelmed by doubt to becoming a brave, dutiful soldier.

a. Wilson's request to have Henry return his letters

b. The cheery soldier's helping Henry find his regiment

c. The selection of the 304th Regiment to "charge" the enemy

d. Henry's anger at the seemingly relentless, untiring fighting ability of the enemy

e. The general's derogatory reference to the 304th as "mule drivers"

Answers: (1) a (2) d and c (3) e (4) a and d

Identify the Quote

1. "Where is your'n located?"

2. "Well," he gulped at last, "I guess yeh might as well give me back them letters."

3. "If they keep on chasing us, by Gawd, they'd better watch out. Can't stand *too* much."

4. "Come on yerself, then," he yelled.

Answers: (1) The tattered soldier. At this point, Henry does not have the courage to answer this question because his wound resulted from his running from battle. (2) Wilson. When Wilson asks Henry to return the letters, Henry begins to regain his confidence. (3) Henry. As Henry's regiment is being organized for a charge, his anger at the persistence of the enemy, at their relentlessness, begins to build. (4) Henry. Henry's regiment is selected for a charge. Henry is the first to respond as he jumps up from his protected position and joins the lieutenant in the charge across the open field.

Essay Questions

1. Identify and discuss the events which brought about Henry's change in attitude from doubting youth to dutiful soldier, and provide evidence from Henry's comments or thoughts as to why you feel that this change will be permanent.

2. Of the images which resulted from Crane's use of figurative language included in this novel, select five of the most powerful, in your opinion, and discuss the impact which these images had on one or more of the following literary elements: plot, setting, characters, theme, or point of view.

Practice Projects

1. View the film version of *The Red Badge of Courage* and compare the changes made in the film (or in the made-for-television version) with the actual text as written. Discuss the effectiveness or the ineffectiveness of those changes.

2. Visit *The Red Badge of Courage* Web site or a Stephen Crane Web site (see Resource Center: Internet for Web site information for both topics). Select a topic which interests you and evaluate the information provided from the site with other information which you have found on the topic. Compare and contrast the Web site's effectiveness in supporting your research with the other information sources which you have used.

3. Read another historical novel associated with the Civil War, e.g., *Gone With the Wind* by Margaret Mitchell, *The Killer Angels* by Michael Shaara, *Black Flower: A Novel of the Civil War* by Howard Bahr, *Cold Mountain* by Charles Frazier, *Shiloh* by Shelby Foote, or *Woe To Live On* by Daniel Woodrell (many other titles are listed at bookseller Web sites), and compare and contrast the characters and themes with the characters and themes in *The Red Badge of Courage*.

CliffsNotes Resource Center

The learning doesn't need to stop here. CliffsNotes Resource Center shows you the best of the best—links to the best information in print and online about the author and/or related works. And don't think that this is all we've prepared for you; we've put all kinds of pertinent information at www.cliffsnotes.com. Look for all the terrific resources at your favorite bookstore or local library and on the Internet. When you're online, make your first stop www.cliffsnotes.com where you'll find more incredibly useful information about Crane's *The Red Badge of Courage*.

Books

This CliffsNotes book, published by Hungry Minds, Inc., provides a meaningful interpretation of Crane's *The Red Badge of Courage*. If you are looking for information about the author and/or related works, check out these other publications.

Colvert, James B. *Stephen Crane*. San Diego: Harcourt Brace Jovanovich, Publishers, 1984. This work is a brief, concise biography of the life of Stephen Crane.

Gullason, Thomas A., ed. *The Complete Short Stories and Sketches of Stephen Crane*. New York: Doubleday and Company, 1963. This work includes all of Crane's short stories and sketches arranged chronologically.

Stallman, Robert Wooster. *Stephen Crane: A Biography*. New York: George Braziller, Inc., 1968. This work provides a comprehensive review of the life and works of Stephen Crane.

——. *Stephen Crane: An Omnibus*. New York: Alfred A. Knopf, 1952. This work includes selected Crane short stories, novels, poems, sketches, and letters.

Stokesbury, James L. *A Short History of The Civil War*. New York: William Morrow and Company, Inc., 1995. This work reviews the entire Civil War in a brief, but informative, format.

Werstein, Irving. *The Many Faces of the Civil War*. New York: Julian Messner. Inc., 1962. This work provides interesting background information regarding selected people and events of the Civil War.

It's easy to find books published by Hungry Minds, Inc. You'll find them in your favorite bookstores (on the Internet and at a store near you). We also have three Web sites that you can use to read about all the books we publish:

- `www.cliffsnotes.com`
- `www.dummies.com`
- `www.hungryminds.com`

Internet

Check out these Web resources for more information about Stephen Crane and his other works.

Stephen Crane. `www.crane.com`—This site has several links related to the study of Stephen Crane and his works and to the novel *The Red Badge of Courage*.

The Civil War. `www.civilwar.com`—This site links to many Civil War topics.

Send Us Your Favorite Tips

In your quest for knowledge, have you ever experienced that sublime moment when you figure out a trick that saves time or trouble? If you've discovered a useful tip that helped you understand Crane's *The Red Badge of Courage* more effectively and you'd like to share it, the CliffsNotes staff would love to hear from you. Go to our Web site at `www.cliffsnotes.com` and click the Talk to Us button. If we select your tip, we may publish it as part of CliffsNotes Daily, our exciting, free e-mail newsletter. To find out more or to subscribe to a newsletter, go to `www.cliffsnotes.com` on the Web.

Index

A

Active Service: A Novel, 4
animal imagery, 23
author
    biography, 2–5
    other works, 4

B

Bacheller-Johnson Syndicate, 3
battery, 24
battle, 21
    brigade watches, 25
    charge, 57–58
    charge, plans for, 56
    death, 57–58
    enemy flag, capturing, 68
    experience, reviewing, 70–71
    Fleming, Henry, 27–28
    forecast, 14, 18–19
    Henry fires relentlessly, 54
    Henry flees second, 30–31, 79
    Henry sees advancing soldiers, 42
    Henry turns back toward, 35, 36
    internal conflict before first, 14–19,
        21–23, 25, 79
    lines reform, 66
    metaphor, 23, 31, 82–84
    nature's contrast, 28, 31, 34, 43
    personification, 23, 31–32, 82–83
    regiment enters, 27
    regiment under duress, 60, 63, 66, 67
    retreating soldiers envelop Henry, 44
    simile, 28, 35, 82–83
    withdrawal, 70
biography, author, 2, 3
Black Riders and Other Lines, The, 5
blacklooks, 53
Bonaparte, Napoleon, 20
books
    author's other, 3–4
    resource, 90–91
brigade, 20

C

calvary, 45
captain, 26
Captain, The, 11, 25, 77
characters
    analyses, 74, 75, 77
    list, 10, 11
    map, 12
    third person terms, 19
Cheery Soldier, 9, 11, 44, 45, 76, 80
chin music, 53
Civil War
    history, 7, 8
    reference materials, 90–91
Claverack College, 2
CliffsNotes Resource Center, 90–91
CliffsNotes Review, 87–89
colonel, 20
color
    battle images, 85–86
    Henry's mental state, 71
    literary devices, 43, 71
    nature images, 31, 43, 45
color sergeant, 26
Commodore, 3
company, 26
company wags, 20
Confederate soldiers, 22, 26, 31, 32, 69
confidence
    criticizing officers, 22
    maturity, 64
Conklin, Jim
    character analysis, 21, 76
    death, 8, 9, 37, 48, 49, 75
    described, 10
Conrad, Joseph, 3
Corporal, The. *See* Simpson
Crane, Agnes, 2
Crane, Stephen
    biography, 2–3
    other works, 4–5
curiousity, 35

D

death, 79
    battle, 57, 58
    Confederate flag bearer, 69
    Conklin, Jim, 8, 9, 37, 48, 49, 75
    fear, 8, 23

NOTES

NOTES

CliffsNotes

LITERATURE NOTES

Absalom, Absalom!
The Aeneid
Agamemnon
Alice in Wonderland
All the King's Men
All the Pretty Horses
All Quiet on the
   Western Front
All's Well &
   Merry Wives
American Poets of the
   20th Century
American Tragedy
Animal Farm
Anna Karenina
Anthem
Antony and Cleopatra
Aristotle's Ethics
As I Lay Dying
The Assistant
As You Like It
Atlas Shrugged
Autobiography of
   Ben Franklin
Autobiography of
   Malcolm X
The Awakening
Babbit
Bartleby & Benito
   Cereno
The Bean Trees
The Bear
The Bell Jar
Beloved
Beowulf
The Bible
Billy Budd & Typee
Black Boy
Black Like Me
Bleak House
Bless Me, Ultima
The Bluest Eye & Sula
Brave New World
The Brothers Karamazov

The Call of the Wild &
   White Fang
Candide
The Canterbury Tales
Catch-22
Catcher in the Rye
The Chosen
The Color Purple
Comedy of Errors…
Connecticut Yankee
The Contender
The Count of
   Monte Cristo
Crime and Punishment
The Crucible
Cry, the Beloved
   Country
Cyrano de Bergerac
Daisy Miller &
   Turn…Screw
David Copperfield
Death of a Salesman
The Deerslayer
Diary of Anne Frank
Divine Comedy-I.
   Inferno
Divine Comedy-II.
   Purgatorio
Divine Comedy-III.
   Paradiso
Doctor Faustus
Dr. Jekyll and Mr. Hyde
Don Juan
Don Quixote
Dracula
Electra & Medea
Emerson's Essays
Emily Dickinson Poems
Emma
Ethan Frome
The Faerie Queene
Fahrenheit 451
Far from the Madding
   Crowd
A Farewell to Arms
Farewell to Manzanar
Fathers and Sons
Faulkner's Short Stories

Faust Pt. I & Pt. II
The Federalist
Flowers for Algernon
For Whom the Bell Tolls
The Fountainhead
Frankenstein
The French
   Lieutenant's Woman
The Giver
Glass Menagerie &
   Streetcar
Go Down, Moses
The Good Earth
The Grapes of Wrath
Great Expectations
The Great Gatsby
Greek Classics
Gulliver's Travels
Hamlet
The Handmaid's Tale
Hard Times
Heart of Darkness &
   Secret Sharer
Hemingway's
   Short Stories
Henry IV Part 1
Henry IV Part 2
Henry V
House Made of Dawn
The House of the
   Seven Gables
Huckleberry Finn
I Know Why the
   Caged Bird Sings
Ibsen's Plays I
Ibsen's Plays II
The Idiot
Idylls of the King
The Iliad
Incidents in the Life of
   a Slave Girl
Inherit the Wind
Invisible Man
Ivanhoe
Jane Eyre
Joseph Andrews
The Joy Luck Club
Jude the Obscure

Julius Caesar
The Jungle
Kafka's Short Stories
Keats & Shelley
The Killer Angels
King Lear
The Kitchen God's Wife
The Last of the
   Mohicans
Le Morte d'Arthur
Leaves of Grass
Les Miserables
A Lesson Before Dying
Light in August
The Light in the Forest
Lord Jim
Lord of the Flies
The Lord of the Rings
Lost Horizon
Lysistrata & Other
   Comedies
Macbeth
Madame Bovary
Main Street
The Mayor of
   Casterbridge
Measure for Measure
The Merchant
   of Venice
Middlemarch
A Midsummer Night's
   Dream
The Mill on the Floss
Moby-Dick
Moll Flanders
Mrs. Dalloway
Much Ado About
   Nothing
My Ántonia
Mythology
Narr. …Frederick
   Douglass
Native Son
New Testament
Night
1984
Notes from the
   Underground

**Check Out
the All-New
CliffsNotes
Guides**

TECHNOLOGY TOPICS

PERSONAL FINANCE TOPICS

CAREER TOPICS